Praise for
The Living Spirit: Answers for Healing and Infinite Love

T0058415

"Sheryl Glick has a passion to connect people to their higher selves to effective powerful emotional and physical healing. Her new book, *The Living Spirit,* engages people in their own transformation through illuminating stories, humor, compassion and wisdom. A much needed book in today's world. Share it with everyone you know!"

—Jackie Lapin
Author of the best-selling *Practical Conscious Creation:
Daily Techniques to Manifest Your Desires*

"*The Living Spirit* is a captivatingly beautiful reminder that we are not alone in our journey as enlightened beings on this earth. Through her own personal life experiences, author Sheryl Glick shows us what we have always felt but often ignore: Spirit lives within each of us, and we are all intertwined in its unbreakable divine grace. With the help of this book, you will have practical, perceptive, hands-on information that is like a personal textbook for your spiritual growth, healing, and awareness. I highly recommend it."

—Dr. Carmen Harra
Intuitive psychologist, author of the best-selling
Wholeliness: Embracing the Sacred Unity That Heals Our World

"Sheryl Glick wants to share what she has found to be true, YOU can change and heal, and it all starts with YES. Say YES to listening, trusting and being guided by Spirit. That's Sheryl's message of hope!"

—Robert Brown
International medium, author of *We Are Eternal*

"It's nice to read a book that reminds us again that spirit is alive and well, out-of-body as well as in-body, and we can communicate with these souls for growth and healing if we open our hearts to receive their love. Thank you, Sheryl, for sharing your informative journey."

—Betsy Otter Thompson
Author of *Walking Through Illusion* and *Love Parent*

"*The Living Spirit* by medium and Reiki Master Sheryl Glick fulfills an urgent need for answers in the spiritual seeker's life. With the current economic circumstances and changing paradigm's shattering current belief structures, this book offers hope, healing strategies, and exemplifies how to turn inward for self-awareness. Enjoyable read!"

—**Dr. Caron Goode, NCC**
Award-winning author of *Raising Intuitive Children*
and the Amazon.com international best seller
Kids Who See Ghosts: How to Guide Them Through Fear

"Sheryl Glick is a star—a light force of indomitable energy of love for life. In *The Living Spirit,* Sheryl takes her readers on a journey of healing, giving us the means for transforming our deepest fears to find within the truth of our individual and collective Spirit. Intensely analytical of life, death, and the human thought process, she explores Universal Energy and how to harness it for our best life."   —**David M. Glick**
Attorney at Law, author of *Title Closing Seminars*

"A wonderful intuitive reading with Sheryl Glick helped free me of a burden that I have been carrying for some time. Sheryl is a warm and generous soul, and her esoteric yet down to earth communications come straight from the heart. I have studied the mind in depth as a psychoanalyst, and the body as a medical doctor, but the spiritual piece is only now beginning to take its rightful place in my life. Sheryl Glick has much spiritual wisdom to offer and I highly recommend reading *The Living Spirit.*"   —**Judy Tsafrir, M.D.**
Harvard-affiliated holistic adult and child psychiatrist
and psychoanalyst in Newton Center, MA

"What Sheryl writes in her book coincides with my extensive study of near-death experiences. We all have divinity within us; we just need to find ways to express it. In telling her own life story, Sheryl displays tremendous wisdom and love. She gives practical advice and techniques to continue going forward. And most importantly, she encourages all of us to follow our own spiritual road to expressing our divinity."

—**Christophor Coppes**
Author of *The Essence of Religions* and *Messages from The Light*

The Living Spirit

Answers for Healing and Infinite Love

Sheryl Iris Glick

SelectBooks, Inc.

New York

Contents

Acknowledgments

This book and all the people mentioned within the pages of this story, whether brought to me by varied coincidences or divine intervention, are now and forever more intertwined within my heart and soul energy and joined in love with my ever-expanding circle of family, friends, mentors, editors, agents, and the multitude of people who have shared their insights, their time, and their stories truly from their heart experience. I thank each and every traveler through time and space who has shared the true measure of our soul and physical lives together, bringing continuous love and wisdom from above to this Earth plane.

For physically making it happen, much gratitude to my agent Pauline Vilain of the Netherlands, who worked tirelessly, selflessly, and led me to know that *The Living Spirit* must be published as the message it offered the world was so necessary during the shifts being experienced all over the world at the present time. Pauline insisted that I accept the offer from SelectBooks in New York and choose Kenzi Sugihara as my publisher. Following her guidance and being sure that SelectBooks was the right publisher, I went forward with this choice and want to also thank Kenichi Sugihara, Nancy Sugihara, and Molly Stern for their work on *The Living Spirit*.

A week after making this decision, I was informed by my editor, Dana Micheli, from Writers in the Sky, that Pauline had passed. Pauline Vilain represented me with dedication, integrity, honesty, and a soul trust in the work we were doing. I hope Pauline watches and shares in the joy of the publication of *The Living Spirit*.

For professional assistance, I thank my agent, Stacey Glick, Vice President of Dystel & Goderich Literary Management; my editors, Dana Micheli and Dr. Caron Goode; my assistant Brooke Chamberlain;

and for professional and creative encouragement, the experienced authors, publicists, spiritual counselors, and medical doctors including, but not limited to, Dr. Eben Alexander, Robert Brown, Master Charles Cannon, Andrew Cohen, Rabbi Wayne Dosick, Rabbi Matthew Gewirtz, Dr. Henry Grayson, Dr. Susan Groh, Dr. Carmen Harra, Dr. Jean Houston, Dr. Brian J. Katz, Dr. Jaime Koufman, Jackie Lapin, Rita Roberts, Gertrude Mark, Steve McIntosh Esq., J. D. Messinger, Dr. Raymond Moody, Associates at Meryl Moss Media Relations Inc., Dr. Renee Messina, Dr. Richard Moss, Dr. Eric Pearl, Dr. Maurie D. Pressman, Dr. Charlene M. Proctor, Dr. Larry Rosen, Don Miguel Ruiz, SQuire Rushnell, Dr. Vernon M. Sylvest, and Dr. Charlotte Tomaino.

For emotional latitude, many thanks to my family: my husband, David; my daughter, Stacey, and my son, Gregg, and their spouses; my grandchildren Samantha, Alea, Chelsea, Talia, Sullivan, and Greyson; my sisters and their families; Nancy M. Barahona, and to my family in spirit: mom and dad, grandparents, aunts and uncles, along with friends, much gratitude. They all have contributed to my developing a strong sense of the joy and love in life.

I am especially thankful to my students and clients who have made a conscious effort to remove the layers and illusion of their lives in search of their inner essence and soul power. How grateful I am for the opportunity to experience life by having my feet in two worlds—the physical and the spiritual, utilizing the sacred Universal Energy that connects my soul to both dimensions. How much better life becomes when we are awakened to the true possibilities of our dynamic and ever-changing eternal soul being.

Introduction

Recognizing Our Spiritual Gifts

My grandfather had been dead for thirty years when one night in 1993 I awoke to find him standing in my room. Before I could speak, he said, "You have to write something for your father." Then he was gone. I sat up in bed, still a bit groggy. It was such a strange dream, I thought, so strange and so *real*. I rarely thought about my grandfather, yet I could actually feel him standing beside me. I had no idea what his words meant, either, until the next day when I learned that my father had passed away. That's when I began to question what had really happened, and whether it had been just a dream. But if my grandfather had visited me in spirit to prepare me for my dad's death and let me know that I would write his eulogy, why had he waited so long to visit me? He had been gone for so many years.

As I joined my family in mourning, I knew nothing would ever be the same for me again. Although I intuitively knew what I had seen and heard was true, it was still difficult to comprehend, and I had no one to speak to about this new world that had suddenly opened up to me. Raised in the Jewish faith, I had always been taught that there is no afterlife, and back then there were no Google searches, local metaphysical classes (at least that I knew of!), or mediums on TV. I spent the next several years seeking out the answers to my many questions, with Spirit guiding me every step of the way through a series of "chance meetings," which I describe in my first book, *Life is No Coincidence*.

A key turning point in my journey happened six years after my father's passing when I was told to read *One Last Time* by the famous medium and fellow Long Islander, John Edward. He described the difference between a spiritual visitation and a dream, and after reading his description I could no longer question what had happened to me. I knew it was indeed a spiritual visitation. I wondered where my grandfather was living now and how I could hear from him again. I started to attend spiritual conferences—including a week-long seminar hosted by John Edward in Barbados—and trainings around the world. In the meantime, I continued to consume every metaphysical book I could get my hands on and speak with every expert I could find about the "Other Side."

As I began to step outside my comfort zone, I realized that there were thousands of people just like me, who had been thrust into a new state of awareness of life beyond the physical plane. Once this happened, it was impossible to go back to that three-dimensional way of thinking. Suddenly the concerns of everyday living like worrying about paying the rent and managing our family and careers was no longer enough. We were seeking something greater; we were seeking the truth of why we are all here and our connection to what is beyond us.

Throughout the amazing journey that followed I learned several truths. The first is that there is indeed an afterlife; the second is that the separation between this world and the next is not a thick, impenetrable wall, but a thin veil that allows our loved ones in spirit to communicate with us, and we with them. We are never alone, but are guided by these loved ones at all times. They assist us in making the choices in this life that prepare us for the next dimension, where we will encounter further support for our soul development in that world. The assistance received from spiritual influences will be in proportion to our wish for help and to the effort we expend in our self-growth process in this lifetime.

I also learned that everything in the universe—including our physical bodies—is made up of pure energy, and that working with this energy can affect a healing that repairs our bodies and allows our souls to move toward greater levels of awareness and expansion. I became more and more fascinated by the different modalities of energy healing, and was eventually guided to begin my Reiki studies at the Association for Research and Enlightenment in New York City.

Today, I am a Reiki Master practitioner and teacher, as well as a medium—albeit a different kind of medium. Before each Reiki session, I go into a meditative state, traveling to other realms and levels of consciousness. The information I retrieve about the client informs the session so that the energy channeled through me goes where it is needed most. As internationally known medium Robert Brown, whom I have worked with over the years, once told me, "It seems you have been touched differently." Perhaps he meant to share with me that mediums or intuitive healers are unique in the way they serve the public and explore their own life issues. As a practicing healer/medium I am able through the channeling of energy and messages to help an individual or a group access their own soul being, leading them to know there is no separation between where we begin as energy beings and physical beings. In reaching a larger audience via writing and the Internet radio shows, and by bringing together a world community of speakers with united messages from the metaphysical realm, the necessary changes to our world community and our evolution will continue.

As an energy healer, I help people discover their own energetic presence. After connecting to their soul, they are often able to perceive new thoughts about long-term fears or limitations that have impeded their progress in a way that allows needed changes to be made. I personally believe that we have destinies, experiences, and challenges that enable us to grow, expand, and evolve. As we learn to feel and manage our energies and emotions, we increase our abilities to deal with all of life's experiences. Each day I awaken with the intention to send and receive the most positive thoughts and to have the greatest adventures, whether for sheer fun or for learning. Each moment is an opportunity to remember I must be grateful to be alive, conscious and comfortable with my own energy, physical body, and spirit.

Through my readings, clients begin to understand their spiritual connections to a higher dimension, where souls who depart their physical bodies now reside and communicate with all souls on the Earth plane: some individuals more sensitive than others are receiving more complex messages. I believe our loved ones in spirit guide us to expand our understanding of our soul nature. They knew us in their physical lives, but after crossing over they may become our teachers, helping us to gain knowledge of life, death, and how to better navigate this three-dimensional physical plane called Earth. There is a universal sphere of continuous knowledge beyond Earth; it is the point where the past, present, and future merge. In reality, there really is no past, present, or future. There is only energy. Even the challenges, no matter how hard, must be experienced in order to understand the strength and power of our divine energetic being.

I aim to empower people who seek to empower themselves and to help them improve the quality of their thoughts by creating well-defined intentions to manifest the best results in their everyday lives. Healing energy sessions are a catalyst for self-improvement and to also improve the quality of interactions with others.

Everyone has spiritual gifts. But for some it is a life purpose, a call to be an extension of God's love in service to humanity. They grow to understand, as I did, how difficult the transition can be from the mind-centered consciousness of this dimension to realizing our true duality as spiritual beings having a human experience.

When people are first called to do spiritual work—whether energy healing, mediumship, or in my case, a combination of the two—it is quite common to doubt whether it is real. In fact, they may even doubt their own sanity. This is exponentially harder when friends and family do not believe what they are experiencing is real. Then, not only do they think they are going crazy, but that they are going to be crazy and *alone*. They don't yet realize that we are never alone, for Spirit is with us always. They may also be confused about the strange physical sensations they are feeling, whether it is hot, tingly hands, or the sense that someone or something not of this world is trying to communicate with them.

I have certainly been there. Before I awakened to the awareness of the continuity of the eternal Soul, the immense possibility for the growth of each person's personal power, and the ability to connect to spiritual energies, I did not know or even vaguely understand how to listen to my inner voice. Was this whisper of guidance from a higher self, or a gut feeling connected to the mind, or an innate cellular intelligence? I now know the inner voice comes to us from our own soul essence, as well as from the Divine whispers of other souls to whom we are connected and who wish to aid us from afar in whatever situations we find ourselves.

The mind, containing our intellect or ego with its constant chatter and fearful thoughts, makes it hard to follow our soul whispers. After years as an energy healer and medium, I am aware of the ordinary mental thoughts as compared to the higher thoughts of my soul and all the souls in Spirit. One may recognize and differentiate a soul thought from a personal thought by how swiftly and intensely it comes into their head.

For example, one day as I was driving to my office, a quick definitive thought came in and said, "Pick up the birthday cake!" I realized it was my responsibility to get Caroline's birthday cake as I had promised. I changed direction and quickly went to the bakery.

These souls who whisper to us may be part of this continuum of Divine energy, or God, and are all working together as our guides, teachers, and guardian angels. Change and growth occur within the mind and physical body, and also within the evolution of the soul or energy body. Growing our physical and spiritual aspects equally in alignment to universal energy is one pathway to fulfilling one's destiny.

Once people begin to realize their dual nature as human beings and spiritual energy forces, a new world of awareness begins to open up for them. It might be compared to stepping into a golden beam of light or knowledge, available to those who willingly avail themselves of this transformative and enlightened state of being. They will begin to realize that not only are they sane, but have been given an amazing gift: namely a means to embrace messages from Spirit and integrate our human experience with the Divine.

In this book I share simple but powerful exercises that I personally use to shed negative energy, resistance, and mental clutter. These exercises and insights can help us to protect ourselves from "energy vampires," people who may try, knowingly or unknowingly, to rob us of our state of joy and well-being. Learning to act proactively rather than reactively may teach us how to respond when family and close friends are not supportive. Perhaps more importantly, I also share incredible stories from my own spiritual journey that will illustrate these points and hopefully illuminate the path for others.

The timing for this book could not be better. For years, the metaphysical community has predicted a tremendous shift in human consciousness, and it is happening now. More than ever, people are feeling the need to rediscover their life's purpose, and the economic downturn in recent years has given many the freedom, opportunity, and necessity to change their lives and work. Energy healing—including Reiki, Healing Touch, Reflexology, Chiropractic Adjustments, Acupuncture, Massage and Body Work, Rolfing, Polarity, Trager, Chromotherapy, Radionics, Alexander, Bioenergetics, Feldenkrais, Deep Tissue Work, Osteopathic Manipulation, and other modalities—has become one of the fastest growing fields of complementary health care, and it is part of my mission to help healers develop their God-given gifts.

I have written The Living Spirit not just for healers, but for anyone who wants to awaken to their soul's mission and to the incredible plan God has for them. It is intended as a compassionate and supportive guide for others beginning their spiritual journey as mediums, psychics, and energy healers or simply for those with questions about who they are, what life is all about, and whether there is indeed life after death. In short, it is the book I wish I had on that night all those years ago.

In gratitude for my spiritual gifts, I made a commitment to live according to the universal laws of energy and to share all I've learned with others. This includes helping others to conquer their childhood fears and limitations so their souls can mature. As our souls grow and expand, our physical lives expand and abound in abundance. It is my hope that by reading the personal stories shared by a host of people and those from my daily life, it will become apparent to you that each of us is more than we appear to be. We can transform our selves and our world into a place that reflects the best of our divine gifts.

When one shifts to living in conjunction with spirit, and to moving through their emotional issues with new vision and expertise, anything is possible. Another major emphasis of this book is to share the miraculous happenings and coincidences that have proven to me, a former skeptic, that life is not random, and all our experiences are the way to a higher understanding of self.

There are three main points that I hope readers take away from *The Living Spirit:*

> We are divine soul beings interconnected to each other and to the universal energy that supports all of us.

> Life is not random. Throughout our lives we will experience a series of "coincidences" that are not coincidental at all, but Spirit, whispering words of love and guidance in our ears.

> Our loved ones in afterlife guide us to expand our understanding of our soul nature and our physical lives.

I invite readers to share this journey with me and learn to let go of any restriction preventing their full enjoyment of life. Once we become aware of how we can recognize and utilize coincidences, synchronicities, and higher guidance, we can begin our exploration of what these mean in our lives and in our role in the world. We all have the Divine-given abilities to repair our wounds and misguided thinking. Through meditation and energy work like Reiki, we can learn to quiet the mind of negative chatter and learn to find that place within where we are sure of God's love and guidance.

1

∞

Journey to Personal Awareness

Give me beauty in the inward soul;
may the outward and the inward man be as one.

—from Socrates' prayer in Plato's *Phaedrus*

As a Reiki Master teacher, I help my students learn and practice energy work so that they may clear themselves and others of negative energy that causes physical and emotional pain. As a medium, I host an unfoldment group that enables them to receive messages from Spirit through the six psychic "claires": clairvoyant, clairaudient, clairsentient (feelings), claircognizant (knowing), clairegustient (taste), and clairscentient (scent). Each person receives information from higher energy differently. They may be stronger in one aspect of communication than another, but as they learn to trust the internal guidance system, they all become aware of higher energy around them that is supporting them, communicating with them, and loving them unconditionally, with no expectations and no judgment. Eventually, and as they are willing to allow it, this energy also teaches them to do the same with the people in their lives.

My role in my work is to assist my clients in realizing that they have ultimate control over their life decisions, while not necessarily over the circumstances that occur. In the moment of awareness, they achieve a sense of completeness and oneness with Spirit that is beyond anything they have felt before. The question is, how do you arrive at this wonderful moment of awareness? How might you begin to let go of the bits and pieces of beliefs imposed on you during your childhood, which in adulthood limits your ability to find fulfillment? By realizing our childhood beliefs and behaviors no longer work for us, we can choose to take responsibility for making positive improvements in thoughts and actions and move past the bits and pieces imposed on us in childhood. Even a child who has a difficult early life can, with the right support, transcend his or her circumstances to find a decent and fulfilling life.

Tuning into Universal Energy and Messages from Spirit

The story of Mary's daughter, Ginny, reflects the triumph of the human Spirit over life debilitating injuries received early in life:

Ginny had come to me for an energy healing session in the past. She had a challenging beginning, but was unstoppable in her faith and zest for life. A truck hit Ginny when she was only six-years-old and according to the circumstances surrounding her injuries, Ginny should not have survived. Mary has always told me that it must have been more than a coincidence that the exact specialist for Ginny's life-threatening injuries was in the hospital the night of the accident.

When Ginny was a grown woman, she married Gary, who also had multiple neurological issues. They happily shared a pure and innocent first love experience, but Gary died unexpectedly at the young age of forty-two years.

Mary brought Ginny to me for a healing session and reading after Gary's passing. During the session, I experienced the deepest feelings of love and peace felt by both Ginny and Gary. These feelings flowed through me, expanding my heart. I knew in those moments that Ginny accepted her great loss because she had great trust in God's plan for her and for her departed husband. Weeks later, Mary reported that Ginny was physically stronger and had registered in some new classes. Eventually she moved out from her mother's house to live on her own.

Several years later, Mary announced to me that Ginny was very much in love with a new friend who had muscular dystrophy. Ginny was soon to be engaged to him. I started to cry. I work on people in my healing practice and most are overwhelmed with ordinary issues. Ginny was blessed to find two souls to truly love. I believe Ginny's mother's great resilience and openness had given Ginny the gift of love. This gift of love could not be defeated by any physical challenge of the body. Love is a feeling of the soul and of the remembrance of our divine essence.

This energy healing session with Ginny was a gift to me from Spirit, for I was able to feel her unwavering sense of compassion and to know God had given her a second chance to have a partner to love and be loved.

Ginny and her family were conscious of the efforts needed by all to assist Ginny in creating her beautiful life. We need the support of loved ones in all our undertakings. It was necessary for all of them to release the chains that bound them to the traumatic events of Ginny's accident. Their fears and living in the past might have dampened the brilliance and full potential of her spirit, but Ginny and her family were able to move forward, inspired to find new ways of creating the best reality for all of them and going beyond her physical limitations.

In asking for assistance and services from the medical community and by utilizing prayer and meditation, their fears were dispersed and their finer thoughts of love and hope were expressed to Spirit and then manifested in their lives. As in any challenging life situation, practicing meditation and asking Spirit for help during that silent time will help us to learn about our life plan, opening the way to a personal understanding and interpretation of what is needed for achieving a life of joy as Ginny did.

In continuing our quest for personal truth, along with our goal to hear the whispers, experience beautiful thoughts, and sense the feelings of peace that may reside in our soul and body, a pleasant feeling of cooperation between body, mind, and soul can be achieved to bring about a future reality of substance.

Reiki energy healing sessions have enabled many of my clients to feel their own flow of energy and to become aware of their intuitive natures. A more comprehensive knowledge of individual assets and powerful life force factors is the payoff for this exploration of self.

Some people believe that spirituality and self-awareness, a connection to the universe, and understanding of life and death are only available to the old and wise, the well-educated, or the affluent seeker and traveler. But in reality, there is no age, race, gender, socioeconomic, or religious requirement necessary to discover who we are and what we want and need for a successful life journey.

Over the course of my energy-healing practice I have worked with children. Often their parents are present when we go over the information so that the parents might gather a clearer understanding of their child's challenges or needs at the moment. Many parents have a limited understanding of what is really going on with their children as children often are unable to recognize why they are not feeling well or are afraid and not able to express themselves adequately.

I remember a child who was brought to me because she was not eating and was dehydrated and sad. During the reading, after hearing an encouraging message from a spirit, the seven-year-old was able to express to her mother, that she didn't like the food her grandmother and aunt gave her when taking care of her after school. We allowed her to guide us and give us suggestions about what she would enjoy eating. The child also said she wanted to spend more time with her mother who was working many hours.

As a result of this session, her mother decided she was able to arrange her schedule to make more time for her daughter. Life improved for everyone in the family. All children need to be secure and close to their family members, but also must find a way to express their personality and individual needs.

Once when engaging in a reading for my granddaughter Samantha, I received an impression showing Samantha holding a dandelion seed pod that forms after the flower fades. As she was blowing the white poof particles into the wind after making a wish, I asked Samantha what her wish was, but she said she wasn't sure. Soon after this, a friend recommended to me Dr. Wayne W. Dyer's new children's book, "I Am." I came to a page that appeared to be the exact image I received of Samantha with the dandelion. The text accompanying the drawing said, "Along the way, you will find great happiness and love, and you'll learn that wishes come true from within, not above."

A week later at a playground Samantha was on a swing flying high into the sky, when she called out to me with a smile. "I just want to be happy." It seemed she had made her wish!

Focusing Our Energies to Create a Good life: The Law of Attraction

Many choose to believe it is life circumstances that are at the root of the destruction of so many fine plans, intentions, and opportunities. I believe, it is the perception of limitation and self-doubt, not our circumstances, which destroys dreams and thwarts wonderful ideas. What I call The Law of Attraction is a universal, energetic truth of creating our own reality by bringing to us the people and circumstances that our mind and actions generate. What we focus our thoughts, time, and energy on—whether knowingly or unknowingly, whether positively or negatively, whether lovingly or hatefully—sets up a ripple of interaction with other people, places, and events that ultimately brings these possibilities into reality. The thought begins on an energetic, mental level and sometimes proceeds after days, months, or years into a manifestation of a concrete reality.

The Law of Attraction* is often defined as the name given to the belief that "like attracts like" and that by focusing on positive or negative thoughts, one can bring about positive or negative results. This belief is based upon the idea that people and their thoughts are both made from pure energy, and the belief that like energy attracts like energy.

Therefore, I propose that you shall receive what you offer to others and what you wish for or ask for continually from Spirit,

---

* "Law of Attraction." *Wikipedia*. Wikimedia Foundation, 09 May 2013. Web. 06 Sept.

and you'll receive what you expect in response to your perception of what is important to your needs. Everything of both a positive or negative nature is often reflected and given back to you by a universal force that does not judge, but simply delivers. "Be careful what you wish for," is an expression that holds enormous accuracy. Universal force only acts on the vibration of our thoughts, so we must carefully clarify our needs, and refine our thoughts before making requests or expending too much energy on an undesirable pursuit. First, we must discover our real values and what truly brings us inner and worldly contentment before we concentrate our thoughts and efforts toward any goal. The universal energetic forces of life are there for each of us to access, but our life choices and actions, not God, actually create our inner and outer experiences.

"Self-discipline is an act of cultivation. It requires you to connect today's actions to tomorrow's results. There's a season for sowing, a season for reaping. Self-discipline helps you to know which is which."

—Gary Ryan Blair,
Author and motivational speaker

Spirit allows us to face challenging situations that our energy (emotions and thoughts) bring into our lives and help us to see that we are on the right or wrong track. Therefore, we are co-creating our life by observing what is happening and by seeing how to make the best of any situation. Through our faith and the surrender of some of our personal needs, we allow the universe and a higher source to help us find new ways to search and remember our already preconceived destiny and life plan. Spirit gives us all the time in this world, in this life and other lives and beyond, to find our greatest means for developing levels of infinite love and healing as evolving compassionate expressions of the Divine.

We can observe that in addition to our ability to heal and change certain patterns that separate us from our natural state of well-being, difficult and tragic events are occasionally the precursors of taking a soul to the next level of their development. Christopher

Reeve and his story of success and triumph over many challenges in his professional and physical life attest to this statement.

Under the Law of Attraction, we instantly sense and revel in that moment of connection. I felt that Christopher Reeve was a soul I was meant to take notice of when I saw him perform very early in his acting career. Later Christopher was perfectly cast in the role of Superman and is remembered for his excellence in that film. When he became paralyzed in a horseback riding accident, I was so saddened by that event, but sensed that he would develop the strength to turn that tragic event into a way to help himself and others.

Several years after his accident, I received a packet of information from Mr. Reeve's foundation containing a post card showing the steps of a Mayan Temple in Mexico. The steps rose up and then disappeared into the soft, endless clouds. I had just shown the same picture in a magazine to my special needs class on the last day of the school year. In his letter accompanying the picture Mr. Reeve said that after his accident he no longer thought his life was worth living. But when a stranger sent him this mystical card, he felt encouraged to reach beyond the limitations of his physical body and find his divine connection to life and God. He then challenged himself, his wife Dana, and his family and staff to begin a crusade of personal excellence to appreciate their lives as they were and to help others to deal with spinal injuries.

I was moved to reach out to him knowing full well he might not see a letter I wrote and sent to him. But I believe he heard my expression of love for his bravery. Within two years after his death, his wife Dana died from lung cancer. I also believe that Christopher and Dana's love and purpose in their life together were so intertwined that in death their two souls found each other and will walk in spirit forever.

We will learn that we can manifest the lives, loves, and relationships we truly want, and perhaps, most of all, we will see our circumstances as something that can assist us in taking our souls to the next level of development.

Throughout my journey, I have learned to pay attention to the connections between my thoughts and reactions as the Universe continues to place amazing teachers and events in my path to teach me how to do just that. Many of the teachers have appeared as guests on my radio show, *Healing from Within,* which I have been hosting for several years. The purpose of the show is to empower listeners to find their own path to spiritual and physical healing, and to this end, I have interviewed some of the most incredible metaphysical experts, religious leaders, and open-minded medical professionals at work today. The knowledge these guests have provided me with has greatly expanded my awareness and improved my own practice.

After interviewing and reading Sara Wiseman's book *Writing the Divine,* where she suggested ways to realize our own needs quickly and decisively, I was able to take The Law of Attraction to a new level. I wanted purely and simply to have the most gifted and knowledgeable people "request" to be on my show without seeking them out as I had to do when the show was first initiated. I asked those in spirit to bring the most accomplished authors and guest speakers to my show. That very same day, I received three requests from amazing people to be on my show. The first was from a spiritual vocalist in England, Lucinda "Bliss" Drayton. Next was Dee Wallace, author of *Bright Light* and Hollywood actress from the epic film, *E.T. the Extra-Terrestrial.* The third was Hollister Rand, medium and author of *I'm Not Dead, I'm Different.* Spirit quickly provided assistance for me to have what was needed for my radio show, as Spirit or the combined efforts of all the many souls assisting me from above. Spirit seemed to agree that to bring together the beautiful, wise voices of leaders in higher consciousness to share their experiences and wisdom might just be good for us all.

Knowing that Spirit could help receptive clients via Reiki and their own self-healing efforts to create better thoughts and conditions for more positive results, I was soon to see a quick and miraculous example of this truism. I was called to assist a young woman create new thoughts about herself, her situation, and her goals. She needed, and was ready, to make changes that would be in her best interest. Now living in New York, she was originally from the South and was estranged from her family. She was also involved in an abusive romantic relationship and working at a dead-end job. These circumstances were the result of her own lack of self-esteem and patterns of behavior from her childhood that had manifested physically, in all areas of her life, causing her enormous pain and suffering. After five Reiki sessions, and with readings, messages, and encouragement from her dearly loved grandmother in spirit, she left her job. Next, she dumped the boyfriend, reconciled with her family, and went home to begin a new career of service to the community.

Not all law-of-attraction responses are as quick and dynamic as this story demonstrates. Many people have baggage or heaviness of heart and soul and must work through issues buried deep within layers of their psyche. To sculpt or reshape a life and find one's destiny, one must first realize joy and happiness is possible, even though others might suggest we were born to suffer and burn. In essence, we are all truly worthy of receiving the goodness of life.

It is difficult, or nearly impossible for civilized people to think that child rapists, serial murderers, or terrorists are worthy of human consideration, but learning to release, forgive, and move on from the evil workings of others' past judgment, limitations, and restrictions allows us to hold the love that has the capacity to bring us a truly good life.

We are each an independent life form and our choices are our responsibility, either nourishing our own growth, or making us needlessly and unproductively ponder the judgments and actions of others. Anything that is less than accepting of others, whatever their condition, allows for separation from our normal state of love. The goal in the search for enlightenment may be recognizing that while not liking the behavior of "bad" people, the Dali Lama and other highly empowered spiritual leaders have reached a level of detachment allowing them to remain in a love-based energy, finding deeper compassion for the flawed human condition. That is the goal in theory.

Our intentions should always concern our own needs, desires, and wishes and we should not imprint our values or desires on other individuals, as they each have their own life path and story to create. We must focus our greatest hopes for what we want to create for ourselves, first and foremost. When making desires or wishes known to the universe, naming specific people should be avoided, as these people might unwillingly be drawn into our scenarios by our strong desires, and it might not be the right time or situation for them. Mistakes in judgment are possible if we have not fully developed the reasons why we desire a certain action or an outcome. Therefore, we should be mindful, considerate, humble, caring. We should always leave our hopes and desires wide open, viable, and unlimited, since a greater reality than originally thought may be possible and provided by universal intelligence.

For example, if a woman—single or married—wishes to improve and or find more intimacy and greater love in the relationship, she must not put out to the universe the name of a specific person she is focused on. Instead, she should focus on the specific qualities of the relationship she would hope to attract and develop the attributes she respects and admires most within her and work diligently on *becoming* the kind of loving person she wishes to attract. We draw to our self what we are. Once again the Law of Attraction works in harmony with our life situations and what responses we are sending out into the world even if we are unwilling or unable to recognize that truth.

Other Universal Energetic Laws are also operating in the woman's situation. To have a clearer vision of all the spiritual energetic laws and how they address your life challenges, you might refer to Dr. Carmen Harra's book, *The Eleven Eternal Principles,* where she so accurately details how the illuminating wisdom of spiritual values and energetic laws aid us in accessing the Divine within for living more consciously in greater harmony with our human values and issues. The laws she enumerates include: The Law of Totality, The Law of Karma, The Law of Wisdom, The Law of Love, The Law of Harmony, The Law of Abundance, The Law of Attraction, The Law of Evolution, The Law of Manifestation, The Law of Dharma, and the Law of Infinite Possibilities. A greater awareness of each law and the utilization of the wisdom offered to our everyday circumstances may well be the balancing force for your best life.

We have been taught in our formal school days to read, calculate, and create through music, dance, art, writing, and verbalization. Yet most of us were not taught to understand the physical law of cause and effect. We were not shown how people's interactions with us affect our physical, emotional, and spiritual well-being.

I believe that a well-balanced, healthy lifestyle requires being surrounded by supportive people and situations that enhance our positive thinking and produce positive results in our endeavors. Even when some forces may disrupt the flow of events, if we are working within the framework of spiritual or higher values, our choices will be wiser, our recovery from any tragedy will be faster, and we will have a chance for a better outcome and a more lasting impact on others. I am not suggesting that forces beyond our control—illness, loss of a loved one, job, home, friend, physical possessions, or even loss of self due to doubt or fear—are not difficult. But by shifting our perspective, we can dramatically shift the outcome of any situation; we can even turn them into a positive force for change in our lives.

It would serve us well to understand how our positive thoughts can bring us more feelings of self-empowerment, self-esteem, self-love, and acceptance and contribute to how our lives unfold. We see that like begets like, positive action begets positive action, and that positive friends and behaviors can allow for more personal growth leading to more internal or soul growth and greatly enhance the way we handle all experiences. In other words, there are no experiences that should ever throw you completely off your game if you are aligned to the needs and values of your inner world.

Taking Responsibility for Our Happiness

A famous quote from Shakespeare's *Julius Caesar* in a speech made by Cassius, the Roman nobleman, made a strong and lasting impression on me. When Cassius was trying to persuade Brutus that Julius Caesar must be stopped from becoming the monarch of Rome for the public's best interests, he said:

> *"The fault, dear Brutus, is not in our stars,*
> *But in ourselves, that we are underlings."*

Since I receive intuitive messages for my clients, many people have asked me, "How can I find peace and happiness in my life?" This is the answer I give them: Before there can be peace and happiness in a person's life and in the world, every person must be responsible to do their own work about acknowledging what needs to change within their attitudes or actions so that they may better relate to the outer world. Finding true happiness and joy is the natural outcome of self-investigation. There are no short cuts. No one can make you happy or unhappy unless you give him or her the power to do that by surrendering or giving your own power away.

It may seem easier to become a victim and align yourself with other unhappy people, making your status or inclusion in a group secure. But this is a copout. Most people want to be loved and accepted by a group, regardless of the cost to their own individual character. Therefore they tell themselves many stories in order to be accepted by others. Many less evolved souls may even choose to blame parents, spouses, or children for any unhappiness they experience or any delays in achieving their immediate goals or desires. However, it is not only by our own efforts and choices that each of us can develop a sense of accomplishment and self-growth, but by recognizing the greater whole of our being and the role we play in creating everything in our lives.

Many seek to be the best they can be and are encouraged to be perfect. They do not allow less for themselves than what others deem to be perfect for them. But since we are always in a state of change, the ideas and wishes of others are not nearly as important as our welcoming the experiences and challenges that surface and handling them to the best of our ability.

We should aim to become a person who doesn't find fault in others, moving past personal obstacles with courage, hope, and faith to find peace. Be free of any influence of others that take that state of mind-peace away from you.

> *"How simple it is to see that we can only be happy now,*
> *and that there will never be a time when it is not now."*
>
> —Gerald G. Jampolsky, MD
> Psychiatrist and best-selling author of *Love is Letting Go of Fear,*
> Founder of Centers of Attitudinal Healing

Recognizing another avenue for finding happiness is possible when we finally admit, "Not only are we not perfect, no one is perfect." We must continue to learn what makes us tick, and what makes others react as they do, but should acknowledge that we can only change ourselves and our outdated thinking by realizing we are responsible for our own actions. The choice to accept others and ourselves with our frailties and sometimes negative behaviors can be hard, yet it is necessary in order to have times when we feel like we are on cloud 9.

We must realize that each person perceives the world according to his or her life experiences, both present and past; therefore, we will never fully understand another's behavior or their reasons for doing things differently than we do. This realization is the key to allowing and accepting everything and everyone without judgment, anxiety, fear, pain, anger, or hate. It is, you will find, the only way for us to experience true contentment while we are on this three-dimensional plane.

Each of us is unique and we are on different karmic and energetic pursuits. As we learn to apply energetic laws and use them more consistently, we will help create a more harmonious world. Those who understand and live by these laws of energy will have less friction and fewer confrontations in their relationships. Individuals practicing the higher laws of spirit may share this expanding wisdom and state of harmony with others and be an influence for change as their behavior and actions exhibit a positive energy state. With great knowledge comes a greater responsibility to exchange these ideas with those who will listen.

The Benefits of Spiritual Transformation

Spiritual transformation is the key to manifesting a better physical experience, period. It is also necessary to attain life achievements that are not only materially advantageous but are a real reflection of your true Divine self.

Coincidentally, spiritual transformation also allows us to find our higher selves and a connection to universal energy. The ultimate purpose for seeking transformation is to be free of the negative or fearful mind-chatter that results from thoughts of imaginary obstacles and the voices of controlling relatives, friends, and business acquaintances who may be enmeshed in physical pursuits related perhaps to the accumulation of material possessions and the survival needs of the root chakra. By seeking deeper knowledge of your soul, your heart energy, and your life's purpose, you automatically begin to remember that you are more than your body; more than the material or physical world: you are part of a higher life force that is eternal and divine.

Connecting to this inner voice, spirit, soul, energy, or essence brings you an innate awareness of how to commit to your educational goals, the people in your life, your hobbies, interests in nature, and the beauty of creation. This ultimately results in a more balanced, peaceful, proactive state of being, as well as more loving interactions with everyone and everything in your life.

By developing a deeper and continuing connection to a higher source and the divine, you will be able to change from reacting to the will and whim of other people's challenges and fears to finding the life that you wish to create.

Nuturing a stronger inner connection to your own energy and a refined sensitivity to body language and energy vibrations emitted by different emotions will make you aware and enable you to protect yourself from inappropriate involvements or making choices that are not in your best interest.

The following prayer shows me how it is possible to go from a state of pain and victimhood to a place of heroic action, positive creation, and acceptance of life conditions. Who would not choose to live a life of freedom from fear and from the negative aspects that limit our quality of health, joy, happiness, and love? Don't we all seek love, health, and prosperity? Don't we all wish we can find it through spiritual transformation and through hearing the whispers of Spirit? Can noticing the coincidences and synchronistic events that are there for each of us every day of our life be a blueprint and map towards new patterns of successful living?

Prayer of Saint Francis of Assisi

Lord, make me an instrument of your peace.
Where there is hatred, let me sow love;
where there is injury, pardon;
where there is doubt, faith;
where there is despair, hope;
where there is darkness, light;
and where there is sadness, joy.

O Divine Master, grant that I may not so much seek
to be consoled as to console;
to be understood as to understand;
to be loved as to love.
For it is in giving that we receive;
it is in pardoning that we are pardoned;
and it is in dying that we are born to eternal life.
Amen.

Beginning Your Spiritual Journey

How do we begin to see, to feel, to know, to hear in conjunction with higher souls, teachers, loved ones, higher vibrational beings, angels, and indeed the voice of God? While New Age and other spiritual books can offer great insight into other people's journeys, no book can replace your own experiential exploration of your Divine connection.

Begin by finding an energy healer who can teach you about how your energy sustains a healthy life force within, and how you can deal with daily life events in a proactive rather than reactive manner. You should also find a spiritual teacher, a yoga practice, a meditation group, a prayer group, or an outdoor physical activity that brings you closer to the beauty and physical vibration of joy in your life, and at the same time assist in opening the heart chakra to the expansiveness of love and life.

Find a friend who resonates with your Highest Good and encourages your search to find healing on a multidimensional level so that you may transform spiritually, physically, emotionally, and mentally.

You can attune yourself to the life force and living force of this planet by being part of environmental groups, charity work, or school projects that teach our young people to respect our resources and to be more mindful of exploiting our God-given support system: the physical planet.

While it is never too late to begin your spiritual journey, it is important to recognize there are people and experiences being brought to you, right now, from that higher dimension. The sooner you awaken to all the clues and messages that are being provided for your enlightenment, the sooner you can continue moving to your best self.

2

∞

You Are Not Crazy

When true self-remembering comes,
one does not want to alter oneself or others;
one somehow rises above their weakness and one's own.
There can be no blame anywhere.
One swallows what is, and becomes free!

—Rodney Collin, *Conscious Harmony*

There can be no "spiritual development" without, as the above quote says, "true self-remembering," for the two concepts are actually one and the same. We are eternal beings, already perfect in our divinity; therefore, there is nothing to develop, only to remember. That said, we must all realize our responsibility for the path of our physical and spiritual lives. We must also respect others' rights to do the same. When I first started practicing energy healing, I often wondered why more people were not coming to me for a session. In awe of the incredible physical and spiritual benefits, I had figured they'd be coming in droves! The longer I practiced it became clearer to me that each person has to make the choice for healing themselves, just as they would have to make any other choice to change their behavior or lifestyle.

I also learned, through interactions with clients, friends, and even my own family, that many people live in denial about the challenging circumstances in their lives. Moreover, most are not even aware that they are often hiding or deceiving themselves. God's greatest gift was the free will to make our own choices, but with this gift comes an awesome responsibility for what we have called forth in our lives. Until we truly accept this responsibility, it is easy to pretend our lives are happening to us; once we do accept our role, we realize the truth: that it's happening for us.

Recognizing Our Life Paths and Accepting the Choices of Others

As observers of our friend's situations, we often see what they are not yet able to see. It is best if we remember to stand back and wait patiently for them to take control of their own decisions, for that is the only way they can have the experiences they need for their soul's development. It is not easy to watch as those we love suffer over their decision-making; but when we inject our own thoughts and desired outcomes into the mix, we are actually doing what's best for us, not them. On an unconscious soul level we may accept this, but then the ego steps in to save the day and alleviate the discomfort—theirs and ours. Why do we do this? The answer is fear! Fear of what others will think of us; fear of being alone; fear of not being in control, or fear of being considered "crazy." We are our own worst enemies when we interfere with others in this way.

Faith, allowance, and acceptance for our life plan, as well as that of others, are necessary if we are to improve both our everyday lives and continue our path of spiritual ascension. As spiritual speaker Sheryl Richardson once remarked, "Controlling is not receiving." In order to receive energy and Divine inspiration from that higher informational band of knowledge, it is necessary to conquer our need to control others, and it is necessary to be honest with ourselves about what we need to do for our own highest good.

Therefore, we must not make any judgments about other people's behavior and actions, and we must not interfere in the way they choose to conduct their lives. Detachment from judgment and a greater expression of love towards those suffering is the best way to help them. By the same token, we must not allow others to make decisions for us and take away our personal power.

There is a pattern and meaning to all things in Heaven and on Earth, and for each human, there are people and events designed to guide us to face fears and negative thoughts so that we can fully realize our most loving selves or the Divine spark of God within. This is what metaphysical people mean when they say that "we are spiritual beings having a human experience." When we are trapped in the third-dimensional thinking of the physical plane, we are concerned with the minutia of life. This life is often a continuous stream of difficult experiences. However, the spiritual being transforms his/her human experiences—including the "unpleasant" ones—in order to increase their soul's vibration. Thankfully, our family, friends, and guides on the other side have placed people in our earthy lives that can help us make the transition.

That does not mean that all our lessons will be easy or all our teachers agreeable, for there are people out there who will disparage, even attack, our own spiritual beliefs. We must understand that their judgments are the result of their own thinking or lack of knowledge at that moment in time. Sometimes it is the most challenging situations and people that allow us to realize that we are not crazy, but growing to a higher spiritual level.

We arrive in this incarnation with our stories partially written, depending on the family we were born into (the family we have chosen before this incarnation), where we are born, our gender, and so on. Our life path already includes many of the experiences and people who will interact with us. During these interactions and growth periods, our free will enables us to make decisions. We each decide how we will deal with the situations that confront us. We can either grow in soul strength and character through thoughtful, loving decisions, or we can regress through negative, destructive decisions. The game plan is already there, but we get to choose how we play, and that determines how much we accomplish—spiritually speaking—in a given lifetime. Since I believe that this is not the only life experience we have had or will have, I also believe there is plenty of time and plenty of opportunities for individual awareness and growth, as well as collective awareness and growth of the general population.

Of course, not everyone agrees with this point of view (these are the "less than agreeable" teachers I referred to). Some people believe that mediums violate religious doctrines. This concerns me, as they are cutting themselves off from their own divinity and gifts. Just as I believe that mediums receive their gift from a higher source, I believe that we all have the ability to connect to God through the higher consciousness of our soul. Each of us can come to understand the Divine energy at work in his/her evaluation, whether through prayer, meditation, or study. It can also happen through a reading with a medium that's committed to empowering others.

Religious leaders can offer their own interpretations and feelings, and we have the choice to follow religious dogma or a different path. Either way, it is up to the individual to find his or her own truth and communication with God. The Divine Force is in us, around us, for us, loves us, and hopes our love for Universal Source will help us achieve a more successful human experience.

I remember a young staff doctor who worked at the hospice where I volunteer. He was also an acupuncturist, and after hearing about the group I teach, he was interested in learning more about energy work. He knew that as a medical intuitive, I pick up information about people's ailments and sometimes feel the level of pain they are experiencing. One day, he suggested to one of the nurses that they use energy techniques, such as Reiki, to facilitate a lessening of pain or self-healing for their patients. "No, thank you," she said curtly, "but if you want, you can study the Bible at my church. That's the only healing I'm interested in."

A little while later, the doctor asked me if I'd show him what I do. We went into the meditation room, where I put on some quiet music. The doctor was able to relax, and I did receive certain intuitive impressions that I shared with him. I felt the doctor was a very active thinker and loved to study new ideas and belief systems, yet he was also disengaged from people who had once been central figures in his life. I also sensed his fondness for horses. He confirmed all this as true, including the fact that he had recently divorced.

We were in the middle of the session when we heard a loud knock at the door. When the doctor got off the table and pulled open the door, we found the same nurse standing there. "Oh, doctor," she said, looking a bit embarrassed (but of course she wasn't), "I am so sorry to disturb you." It may have seemed like a coincidence, but I know that doubt, judgment, and prejudice often rear their ugly heads to impede progress. Of course, that is a lesson in itself. The young doctor must have agreed, for the next time I visited this hospice unit, I discovered he had left for a new position.

Sometimes we find the most resistance among those closest to us. Most of my own relatives are grounded in the practical aspects of life, and it's difficult for them to let go of antiquated belief systems and consider the idea that energy, thoughts, and all our memories survive even after leaving the physical body. My cousin, Erica, on the other hand, is more receptive to these spiritual ideas, so I felt comfortable relaying a story about her mother, my Aunt Gladys, who had passed away some years before. Aunt Gladys had been coming through with humorous messages at my unfoldment group.

After I finished telling Erica this, Erica told me about a coincidence that she specifically asked me to include in this book. Her middle son, Justin, had been born on her father's birthday. Her father had passed long before Justin's birth. Now thirteen, Justin would have his bar mitzvah on the 12th of January, which was her mother's birthday. Erica felt—and I agree—that these two important dates were signs that Justin still had a connection to his grandparents in spirit. The fact that her mother was also coming through to me brought the "coincidence" full circle. Gladys was reaching out to let us know she is still around and still loves her family. Most of us have experiences like these, but dismiss them as "crazy." When we do this—or allow others to do it to us—we disconnect from our loved one in spirit and their messages.

Connecting to Infinite Love in All Its Forms

In order to embrace our connectedness with our loved ones in spirit, we must also embrace the oneness of all creatures. My experiences are not merely a collection of coincidences and synchronicities, but proof that we all spring from the same Divine Source and are all part of the same Divine story. Yet this realization is only one part of our earthly education; the other part is learning to feel—and generate—a great love for life. This Divine spiritual awakening, and feeling real love without expectations or controls, is very different from what I experienced earlier in my life thanks to my incessant need to achieve, be perfect, and be in control.

After realizing that my life was the result of my choices, as well as the result of the Divine plan I was born with, I have surrendered many of my illusionary fears and asked Spirit to direct and guide me towards the fulfillment of my spiritual purpose. In the process, I have encountered many dear souls who I not only love, but feel have been connected to me in previous incarnations. Of course, I still possess human frailties and, at times, have misinterpreted thoughts. However, I hope to continue, in small increments, to develop unconditional love for others, without expectations. Doesn't every human heart seek love without judgment? When we can accept each other, with all our earthly limitations, without wanting to change, "fix," or blame each other, then a greater sense of peace and freedom will be established.

Over the past several years, I have become free enough of the material world and close enough to the spiritual world to realize these truths. I'm willing to accept the consequences of my actions, regardless of how other people feel or think. I say "no" if it doesn't feel good or right for my development. Even after a lot of study and hard work, this is sometimes hard to do. Nonetheless I strongly believe that this is how the soul matures. I believe just as strongly that it is the mission of all spiritually conscious individuals to help *empower themselves* to share their creative soul expression as they walk their own soul path.

Through meditation and practicing Reiki, I have enabled my intuitive abilities to expand to the point where I now see and feel a dimension beyond this earthly plane. That is how I know beyond the shadow of a doubt that we are all part of God's spiritual energy. It is also how I know that the most ennobled and enlightened souls walk with us, sharing messages of love and joy to all who are ready to hear them. If one can hear or sense spiritual energy and incorporate it into their daily lives, they will find everything about their life immeasurably better.

The first, and arguably, the ultimate goal for those committed to spiritual growth, is to feel complete love for themselves and then extend this love to other human beings. While this may sound simple and even a bit obvious, the practice itself can be quite difficult and can take years, or perhaps forever, to achieve. This unconditional love requires surrendering the false realities offered from a limited material view of the world. But it is this ability to find love everywhere and in everyone which allows the soul to connect to a higher knowing, namely, that all that exists on this and other dimensions are miraculous and infinite.

This is the journey of the soul, and in order for soul maturation, one cannot allow oneself to be any more attached to one soul than others. This can also be hard to accept, let alone implement. After all, aren't we all taught from birth to love our families beyond all else, and to "take care of our own"? Although all expressions of love are equally needed and valued by Spirit, it is in the oneness of being and the fairness to all that means we are detaching from the human ego and have come into the fullness of our divine soul energy. Many of us will not come to this understanding in one lifetime. This is why our marriages, friendships, and other interactions are needed as a vehicle for people to learn from each other.

Even couples who are not well matched energetically, and who have very different patterns and ways of expressing their uniqueness, can learn much about themselves from the other person. In each relationship because of diversity, one may be able to reaffirm their own truth and make any changes to their lifestyle that could significantly be better. Even in troubled or challenging partnerships, recognizing one's own part in the less than satisfactory interaction can help correct personal thoughts and actions and allow the acceptance of differences, clearing the way for a better relationship. When each party is able to respect and allow the other to be who they are and realize their own individual soul goals, a greater universal and divine love is shared.

Opportunities for more loving experiences may even surface from the failure or dissolution of malfunctioning relationships. When we expand our feelings of cooperation, we interact with a higher consciousness, thereby opening the doorway to better relationships in the future. I heard Celine Dion sing the song *Nature Boy,* originally composed by Eden Ahbez. The lyrics that stood out to me most were "the greatest thing you'll ever learn is just to love and be loved in return."

This has been one of the greatest challenges I have faced in my spiritual growth. In the physical world, it is hard for most people to show love for each other without wanting something in return. However, this is egocentric thinking. In order to overcome it, we must silence the battle within for control over others and learn to control ourselves before we can be free of the concerns and emotions of the physical world, such as worries about our survival and common feelings of greed, anger, and jealousy and loss of any kind. But to do so, we must recognize and explore any past fears that inflicted wounds to our loving souls. These fears cause us to approach new situations reacting in the same way as before and facing recurring negative consequences.

Unless the fear is released, we continue the same pattern of action and reaction that bring about continual unwanted and unproductive behaviors. Indeed, I have learned as a result of deep meditation practices and the messages received from Spirit, that the giving and receiving of love is the major reason a soul welcomes a physical life. In one way or another, all interactions revolve around being able to extend past our fears and the fear of losing love so that we can be more loving regardless of how the other person responds.

The giving of love may not necessarily include grand gestures; rather, it is communicated through glances, words, music, undivided attention and concern, and the time invested in others. While this applies to romantic love, it applies to all other forms of attachments as well. If we ask the Divine power to bring us greater love, that is the first step towards achieving it. Being ready to give and receive love is a process of intent and action. Insist on saying what you mean, and mean what you say, as this is your expression or clarification of what is most important to your soul and furthers the refinement of your character.

In addition to being fearless in showing your passions, a person must also be willing to pay the required price for following their goals and dreams. If your pursuits or actions are not always respected by others, this may be a result of their lack of awareness or incorrect timing. While it is sometimes hard to dance to your own rhythm, it is the first step toward living a mindful and soulful existence and understanding love in its many forms.

I once saw in a magazine a picture of a man and a woman on a mountain looking at the vista through binoculars. The thought of love that went with it was: "Love does not consist in gazing at each other, but in looking outward together in the same direction" (from Antoine de Saint-Exupéry, *Wind, Sand and Stars*). Everything I have learned has told me that this is an undeniable truth.

Loving Humanity in Spite of Our Beliefs That Separate Us

Loving all of humanity is made even more difficult by the man-made inventions that seek to separate us. While we can be separated by political or socioeconomic differences, there has been no more divisive an issue than religion. Please do not take this as a disparagement of religious beliefs. Only when we use our beliefs to exclude others, then we may be ignoring the central message of God and his messengers: that we are all connected to Universal Energy and to each other.

I was reminded of this when I saw Mel Gibson's movie *The Passion of the Christ.* I had been looking forward to the movie because of my own growing awareness of the true meaning of the Christ Consciousness, which, like The Ten Commandments given to Moses centuries before Christ, became a philosophy for self-love and love for others. Both, the Christ Consciousness and The Ten Commandments are intended for all people and are the heartbeat of any religious or spiritual message. Indeed, I had always enjoyed Gibson's movies. Years before, my son Gregg had auditioned for the part of his son in another movie. Even though the casting agent told me that no one looked more like Mel than Gregg, he did not get the part. Years later, at a professional film screening, my daughter Stacey and I almost collided right into Mr. Gibson.

This new film, which depicted the last few days of Jesus's life on Earth, promised to become a hotbed of controversy, so in the interest of keeping an open mind I made it my business to see the movie the day it opened. In my opinion, it was not anti-Semitic, as some groups had judged it. The movie depicted the beauty of Christ's love for the Heavenly Father, who asked him to complete his destiny, which unfortunately included his need to experience a physical death at a young age when he had so much to offer the world.

Jesus did not sacrifice his life, but gave it willingly for the greater good of all. Human suffering, whether physical, emotional, or spiritual is a separation from love, honor, courage, and freedom that every soul holds within them. I would hope we would seek the more humane and divine aspects of ourselves, and then move away from all fear and separation to love. But still, until that is accomplished, suffering exists and it is only with greater love that we may conquer it. Jesus's experience was necessary for future generations to realize that personal sacrifices were often necessary for all of humanity to advance and realize God's plan for us. As Jesus faced his departure from Earth, I can only imagine how he might have been frightened in surrendering to the transformation that awaited him. In the movie, Jesus showed human fear and also a soul's acceptance of God's will.

I have seen brutality, barbarism, and the ugly side of human nature in other movies, as well as in real life situations. In stories, war scenes, and clashes between ancient cultures, the depravity of these fights and unprecedented prejudices were simply crass. However, the film's images of the beating, lashing, and bloodying of Christ, not to mention the humiliation of his body and spirit, was beyond everything I have observed. It still seems unbelievable to me. How could any human being even imagine, much less act out, such violence?

Yet the film, for the most part, was an accurate depiction of the stories we have all heard about how his life ended. That said, the movie was also about how Jesus lived before his arrest. It flashed back to the time he spent with friends and followers, showing his gentle nature and his reverence for God and all living things. I believe the movie's message was to help instill a sense of awareness of a larger truth: we are born to complete our life plan, our destiny ... to learn to love and to have compassion for God, man, and nature, and this allows a clearer understanding of the reason for a physical life on this glorious planet. So our soul creates opportunities, which enable us to reach into the depths of our inner being and to bring light into any darkness or destructive situation. These situations of depravity exist so that we might reconnect to an element of light that flows through us in the form of divine energy, compassion, and understanding.

So while I was appalled by the violence, I chose not to focus on it. To me, it was more about the love of a mother for her son and for God. I sought to understand the deep sensitivity felt by one human so long ago, when there were many who could not see Jesus's vision of self-love and love for humanity. Jesus left a vision for the ensuing generations to follow his life, understand his human fears, and his Divine connection.

For several weeks, *The Passion of the Christ* seemed to be on everyone's lips. The day after the movie, I stopped at Dunkin' Donuts.

While waiting in line, I talked to a woman. She felt much the way I did. At the bank, I heard the girl behind me talking about the Jewish involvement with the death of Jesus. It is true that the Rabbis went along with the Romans. Both groups, due to the political climate, made many people, the Jews included, afraid to support anyone indicted by the powers that be. When we spoke, I told her that I was Jewish, and had not found the movie to be an attack on the Jews, but probably an accurate depiction of violent uprisings and the reactions by different political and religious groups of that time period.

But what I found most disturbing was that two thousand years later, the world is still fighting over religious and political issues, land, money, and power. The players are different, but the mentality of the masses is still not representative of the ideals that Jesus expounded. Yet, there are some people who represent a loving, caring, compassionate way of settling discrepancies. We could always use more of these people and there is most certainly room to hope for continual change and progress.

After finishing my banking, I returned to work with my conversation with the woman still on my mind. I realized that the movie would get people to talk and think, just as the horrific tragedy that befell the Twin Towers had stirred conversation and deeply touched the emotions of so many people around the world. Perhaps through dialogue, I thought, people could find new understanding of what Jesus lived and died for. Like other enlightened souls throughout history, Jesus believed in the solidarity between all brothers, all races, religions, and sexes.

These thoughts led me to the ideas of forgiveness and relinquishing pain, as Jesus did when he said, "Forgive them, Father, for they know not what they do." As Jesus had to rise above his agony and forgive his persecutors, so we must also do that in order to bring true peace and harmony to ourselves and to the world. This includes forgiving those among our friends and family who ostracize us for our metaphysical views, for they too "know not what they do."

As I rushed into the office for my next appointment, I literally ran into Sharon, a new massage therapist, energy healer, and psychic. She revealed to me that she had lost her father the previous week. I expressed my condolences for her loss. Just then, the client, who had lost his son on the same day that Sharon's father passed away, walked in the door. Helping someone who has recently experienced such a loss is always difficult, for while I sincerely believe we will be reunited with our loved ones, I also realize this is little consolation at the time of a great loss. For a father who has just lost his twenty-four-year-old son, the thought of seeing him in years to come in the afterlife was unlikely to be enough of a promise to bridge the pain and agony of the moment.

Forgiving anyone, including God, for this kind of loss is unspeakably hard. In spite of this, it is still critical for us to move forward with our spiritual journey. This is true regardless of the circumstances. To this day, I sometimes have to draw on my own reserves to forgive people for whom I had high expectations. Those who don't live up to their own potential sadden me. There are people I know who can be helped by a Reiki session to release painful life issues and create a better life for themselves. However, if they choose not to avail themselves of that service, it is their choice. As my reality differs from theirs, so does the way I choose to face life's challenges. We all have free will to make decisions, even when those decisions might be damaging to our progress.

As for me, I try hard to forgive myself for being unable at times to hold back information that I intuitively sense could help a person in need. But I know not all people are ready or able to embrace advice, and unless asked, I should let the experiences of others play out exactly as they are occurring. Some people may not be ready to take steps to change any experience or their lives.

When we find that our decisions, beliefs, and desires are in conflict with another's, we must simply work through the emotions without allowing them to dampen our spirit. Boundaries must be established personally and in regard to others to safeguard everyone concerned. This includes making a conscious choice to limit our exposure to people who are of a lower vibrational nature or on a different life path while also learning to remove oneself from inflammatory situations. This allows one to be an observer, rather than a participant, and to encourage others to work out their own solutions to their problems.

I now encourage myself to offer less advice and to focus only on positive thoughts and behavior. This has enabled me to embrace wholeheartedly experiences where I can be with others who seek joy, knowledge, and growth as do I. I have learned many practical ways to ground my energy (discussed in chapter 7), so I do not feel as acutely the hurtful sting of negative emotions: the anger, greed, jealousy, and distrust emitted by unhappy people. Most important- ly, I try not to allow energetic inconsistencies to imprint on my sen- sitive feelings or diminish my love of life.

It is my mission to help others in their journey, so that they are able to trust themselves enough to connect to their higher ener- gy. Through my Reiki sessions, I assist them (to the point that they are ready to receive) in letting go of any negativity that resides in their thoughts and actions. Negativity in any form creates a lower vibration that hinders any chance for evolution. It has been docu- mented that about 50 percent of our thoughts, on any given day, are negative and also around half are positive. It is possible with prac- tice to recognize negative thoughts and dismiss them.

At the same time, it is understood that there will always be peo- ple who choose to hide from their problems, whether out of fear, ignorance, or simply not knowing an alternative way. Perhaps they feel the darkness around them because others have acted towards them inappropriately and harmfully. They may believe that keeping secrets and avoiding change will shield them from issues they can't face at the present time. In actuality, only going towards the light and full truth can bring peace, harmony, bal- ance, and the end of suffering. As we cannot change the way any- one thinks or acts, even those that we love the most, we can change our way of interacting with them. And this is an important soul discovery for each of us, regardless of our race, religion, or socioeconomic status.

Methods for Overcoming Fear
or Skepticism from Others

Take It from Whence It Comes

When someone is not supportive of your spiritual growth, recognize he or she is closed-minded, fearful, and living in a state of ego where only their own viewpoint is valued and identified. This person may be a friend or relative with whom you are close. It is in your best interest to allow others their own thoughts and behavior and not take their remarks personally, recognizing they may be in pain and do not have the means to lift themselves out of their limited mindset. Once you realize that it is a reflection of their spiritual state, not yours, it will be easier to forgive them and continue your own journey without worrying that you'll be seen as "crazy."

Take It with a Grain of Salt

Many people gravitate toward bad news, anxiety, and fear, rather than positive thoughts. With humor and goodwill, tell them you understand their viewpoint and request the same respect for your own ideas, if you have the opportunity to respond at all. Then simply continue creating and expressing your own joy. When you hear someone saying, "I didn't get paid enough for the work I did," "My husband, siblings, or parents ask me to do things I don't want to do," or "I have no time for myself or for what really engages my interest," remember that sometimes these are just excuses for not moving forward and doing what they can and should be doing for their own growth. Your joy reminds them of this and may elicit negativity in the form of judgment and skepticism about your spiritual work. (Hint: this is also a reminder to assess and own up to your own lack of motivation. This will help you rethink, reprocess, and bring in the thoughts necessary to create the outcome you desire.)

Take a Stand

Without engaging in arguments with those who oppose your thoughts and actions, simply and unemotionally state your needs and what you will not compromise on. For example, your parents suggest you go to a school to study liberal arts because your other siblings did. However, you know you must go to Parson's School of Design to be with the people who will drive your creativity and where you will find a career that will fit your talent and interests. Keep calmly and passionately sharing your ideas, and if you cannot get them to understand, perhaps find a grant, scholarship, or job that will allow you to proceed with your destiny.

Take the High Road

Many of us struggle with difficult family members who, although related to us, may have a very different view of the world or of a particular issue. To avoid being dragged down by difficult relatives, you must first acknowledge where they are in their journey. Then make it clear that you understand what they are feeling and thinking and that while you respect their decision, it is quite different from your own. The key is to remain nonjudgmental and say no more than what needs to be said.

Take a Dip

In his book *The Hidden Messages in Water,* Dr. Masaru Emoto discusses his experiments with energy and water. Dr. Emoto used a microscope to examine water molecules that had been exposed to positive loving words, as well as those that had been exposed to dark, destructive, and negative words. The positive words created beautiful molecular structures, while negative words created incomplete and chaotic structures that are found in malignant tumors. Remember this when you are interacting with someone who treats you with skepticism, toxic language, and disrespect for your humanity. If you internalize their attitude, it can weaken your immune system and, over time, create illness. We can recognize these people, send loving thoughts and prayers, but then we should, as much as possible, remove ourselves from further interaction with them.

Take Up Reading

Regardless of what other people expect of you or challenge you with, you might remember the two simple words uttered thousands of years ago which continue to provide us with guidance: "Know thyself." Numerous sages such as Pythagoras and Socrates proclaimed that self-awareness is the most valuable of all human qualities because it informs all our life choices and decisions in education, careers, and relationships. It is the defining force of a life worth living. Dan Millman, a former guest on *Healing from Within* and author of *Way of the Peaceful Warrior* and *The Four Purposes of Life*, has reminded me of what I share with others on a daily basis. It is not in the doing but in the becoming that we step over the restrictions, fears, and skepticism of less-evolved friends, family members, and associates to honor the calling within our soul to live a fruitful and dynamic life experience.

Dr. Carmen Harra, author of *Wholeliness* and many other books, writes that "In a sense all of us are clinging to things that are not serving us or giving us pleasure; rather, they're simply cluttering up our lives or weighing us down." These include belief systems, relationships, jobs, and places that may be restricting us from the next step of our development. As we take the leap of faith to make changes away from other people's vision of us, our work, our levels of joy, we are encouraged to "know thyself" and find more satisfaction in all our interactions, even with people who do not understand us.

Take a Lesson from Your Spiritual Masters/ Religious Leaders and Texts

Forgive those who offend or slight you in word or deed, for in forgiving them you allow yourself to be in a state of grace and personal alignment to higher Spirit. Your act of forgiveness frees you to find your own inner peace.

Take a Leap

Embracing new opportunities can be intimidating. However we must remember that the very reason you are being presented with them are for your own spiritual growth. The next time you are tempted to turn down that challenging position or potential romance, stop and ask yourself why. If the answer is a negative or limiting thought about yourself, recognize that Spirit is giving you this experience to help you stretch your spiritual wings, as well as improve your life on this plane. When the fear starts to creep in, try to focus on the journey, not the outcome. You might not stay at the job, and the relationship might not work out—what is important are the lessons you learn along the way.

3

∞

Developing
Your
Mediumship

There is something in every one of you that waits,
listens for the sound of the genuine in yourself,
and if you cannot hear it, you will never find
whatever it is for which you are searching ...

—Dr. Howard Thurman
"The Sound of the Genuine"

Whether you realize it or not, everyone receives messages from Spirit. These messages can take several forms: visual, olfactory, or auditory. Mediums are no different—each receives messages in ways that are unique to him or her. The key is learning how to recognize these messages and begin to uncover your personal "system" for communicating with Spirit. But first you must work on becoming a clear channel for those messages, which essentially means quieting the egocentric mind chatter that can muddy and even block a connection with the Divine.

Some mediums know about their gifts from a very young age. Many, however, are not aware of their gifts for most of their lives. They go about their daily business, paying bills, raising their kids, praying for help, all without realizing that their friends, family, and guides on the Other Side are feeding them a constant stream of information.

This is how it happened for me, for the most part. I remember as a small child crying and wondering why I was "dropped here."

43

Clearly, I yearned for my real home, the Spiritual realm, rather than this harsh, earthly plane. But then I grew up, and as most people do, I allowed myself to be indoctrinated with the third-dimensional thinking—the worries, the fears, and the negativity. That is not to say I was unhappy; I married a young lawyer named David and had two wonderful children, Stacey and Gregg. We lived in an English Tudor home that reflected my love of architecture and history and brought me much joy. I also had successful careers as a teacher and a businesswoman; I studied interior design. I was simply concerned with the physical world, rather than the Divine, during the earlier stages of my life. It wasn't until the eve of my father's death that my grandfather materialized before me, warning me of the coming sorrow and opening up a miraculous new path.

Interpreting the Messages from Spirit

Once I began my investigation into the spiritual world, I realized I had quite the learning curve. One of my "assignments" was to learn how to interpret the messages I was receiving from those on the Other Side. When we are uncovering these messages, it often seems like we are fumbling in the dark, and in some ways we are. It's like a new language—a language of energy vibrations. The important thing to remember is that even if we feel lost, Spirit is always right there, guiding us. Sometimes they might even make it easy for us. As I mention in my first book, *Life Is No Coincidence,* this is what happened with my mother and me.

Like the rest of my family, Mom was not exactly receptive to the idea of an afterlife. She was even less receptive to the idea that I was communicating with Spirit. As a Jew, she was always taught that "dead is dead." However, when she was nearing the end of her physical life, she indicated to me that she was starting to consider the possibility that we do live beyond this earthly plane. I was stunned when one day she said to me, "We are never, never alone." At first I thought perhaps Mom had read a book I had told her about, Michael Berg's *The Way: Using the Wisdom of the Kabbalah for Spiritual*

Transformation and Fulfillment. But as her health continued to deteriorate, I thought maybe Spirit was reaching out to her, letting her know they would be there to guide her to the spiritual realm. Either way, I finally felt comfortable speaking to her about my beliefs.

Shortly before she died, Mom and I made a pact: whoever passed first would send a message back to the other. She chose three doves as her special symbol, and sure enough, after she passed, Mom used it several times to let me know that she was safely on the Other Side. This not only brought me immeasurable comfort; it also reinforced my belief that Spirit uses references from our lives to send us messages.

To this day, Mom uses doves to "check in" with me. One night, while I was watching television with my husband, David, an advertisement for three music CDs appeared. Each CD cover had a dove on it. Mom knew I listened to this type of music to clear my mind, raise my vibration, and enhance creativity.

> *"In everyone's life at some time our inner fire goes out. It is then burst into flames by an encounter with another human being. We should all be thankful for those people who rekindle inner spirit."*
> —quotation often attributed to Albert Schweitzer

Since my mother's passing, I have learned to trust Spirit is sending the right symbols and messages that can be shared with others, helping them in any situation. At a child's birthday party I met Donna, who had recently lost her husband. He was a volunteer firefighter who had survived the horrors of the September 11th attacks only to die in a boating accident shortly thereafter.

A year later, I received confirmation from another medium and was instructed to deliver the message to Donna. Not only was her husband safe on the Other Side, but around to help her adjust to life without him. Just before seeing Donna for the second time, Robert Hansen, a local medium, gave me a message from her husband. The reading also included several of my family members. Hansen sensed a young man jumping in the water to save an older man. My own father had come through during this reading, as well as my first boyfriend, Ira. All three men were standing together, though they had never known each other while alive. As I told Donna the story, I immediately realized that Donna's deceased husband had been her first love, just as Ira had been mine.

I realized that my father and Ira had shown up so I could make this connection of first love and therefore more fully understand the enormity of Donna's difficulty in adjusting to the loss. How wise Spirit was in showing this message to me! Donna asked me if it was worth staying in this life, with all its sickness and hardship. Without hesitation, I told her that I did believe life is a precious gift, no matter the challenges. I remembered the words my mother had said to me after her three-month hospital stay: "Life was good. I have known love." Life, with all its challenges, offers us endless opportunities to have relationships with others and to expand our understanding of love and Spirit. One can often find a moment of grace, courage, and love, even in a time when so much seems to be lost.

While speaking with Donna, I had the distinct impression that there would be another partner for her. She was meant to live life with her husband so she could know the closeness and beauty of first love. After this loss, however, she would understand and appreciate a different kind of relationship. She would experience a mature relationship of the soul. As difficult as it is for us to understand at the time, every relationship, whether ended by divorce or death, was only meant to last as long as it did. No relationship is a failure, as all relationships are preparations for the next experience. Love, even when it ends unpleasantly, is still registered by the Universe as love and is never lost. Furthermore, our loved ones in Spirit sometimes help us to make new connections and bring us greater awareness of true love.

The following story shows how two fathers in Spirit bridged time and space to help their children find each other.

I flew to Miami with my yoga teacher, Pam, and her group to embark on a cruise for five days to the Bahamas. While I waited to embark and go to my stateroom, the steward directed me to the cafe lounge for lunch. A gentleman approached the table and asked in a British accent if he might sit. His wife joined him and I felt it was the second marriage for both. Their names were Amy and Richard. They lived in New Jersey and also owned a house in Montauk on Long Island. They were tall, energetic, and well matched in physical appearance and energy.

In conversation, Amy mentioned she was interested in mediums and how they retrieved information from Spirit. I mentioned that I had recently published a book and was interested in spiritual communication, coincidences, and synchronicity. When Amy asked if I was a medium, I explained my work as an intuitive healer and medium. She asked for my card and said she had heard of me.

Amy is a true believer that everything happens for a reason. It immediately became clear to me that my meeting with Amy and Richard would have an unusual twist of fate. They both worked for different companies in different countries that held national conventions in Japan several times a year. Richard traveled from his company in England and Amy left from the United States. They met and continued to build a relationship. Their long-distance working relationship led to better conditions for the companies they worked for and eventually to their marriage, even though there were challenges in a long-distance romance. True synchronicity is the fact that they met at all and soon found they shared an amazing connection.

Amy told me of an unusual coincidence. Amy's father was in the Italian Army during World War II and was taken prisoner in Ethiopia. He was sent to a farm prison in England. Richard's father ran that prison facility, and the two fathers knew each other well. Both had passed recently and were in Spirit, and Amy believed they had orchestrated the events that led to Amy and Richard's meeting. It seemed that cooperation from the spiritual realm created a fulfilling and better destiny for them.

Guidance from Loved Ones in Spirit

Many of my most treasured experiences have occurred while working in hospice care, perhaps mainly because I have witnessed people, so terribly ill in this life, being greeted and escorted to the next dimension by their loved ones in Spirit. One day, I visited a young woman, Marie, who was having trouble breathing. She was also deeply embarrassed about having all the people there taking care of her. I held her hands and said, "We are all in this life together, and today we will help you, and tomorrow you will help another."

I remembered how I once thought that I had to be independent and never ask for help. As my soul transformed and matured, I learned that we may ask the God-force for whatever we need. There is no shame or guilt in asking God or anyone else for help. God expects us, as his beloved children, to be dependent on him at times. By trying so hard to distance ourselves from love, we create needless pain and suffering.

Still, I understood how such an independent young woman like Marie would be saddened and discouraged by her physical weakness and illness. I asked her mother, Anne, if we could just sit quietly together for a while. She said yes, of course, and within a few minutes Marie had fallen into a peaceful sleep. With my eyes closed, I sensed a grandmother in Spirit standing in a golden, sun-filled grassy area, and I instinctively knew Marie loved the outdoors. I also received a number of other impressions that Anne confirmed as accurate. Anne believed that our loved ones were not gone, just waiting for us on the Other Side. Now she seemed to know that loved ones remained near her daughter and would be with her when she passed.

Anne then told me that her own mother, now deceased, had once had a near-death experience. Upon her mother's awakening, she told Anne that a well-dressed man in a wheelchair had come to her hospital room and invited her to take a plane ride to California (during the near death experience). He had shown her a field of tall grass that swayed in the soft breeze. There was one large red flower in the distance. He told her she could come and live by that beautiful spot when she was ready. It seemed to me that Anne's mother had had an encounter with a Spirit guide. Anne had never told another person about her mother's vision.

Years later, when Marie was ready to be married, Anne's mother appeared to Marie in a dream. Marie told her grandmother all the details for the upcoming wedding. When it was time for her grandmother to leave, she asked Marie to look out the window. Marie saw tall grass swaying in the breeze, and a large, single red tulip in the distance. Upon awakening, she called her mother and told her the story. Then Anne told Marie what her grandmother had experienced before her own death. The description of the place and the flower were one and the same!

For me, this was proof that a place of beauty awaits us if we have positive thoughts and display positive actions during the course of our lives. We may manifest our quality of life in the next dimension by our actions in this life. The choice to walk in light and truth or to shroud oneself in a cloak of fear and darkness is up to each individual.

Now Marie was in hospice care, waiting for her time to cross over. Before I left her room, Anne mentioned how strong Marie's religious convictions were. She had told her mother about a dream she had years before. In the dream her husband was on the beach with her. Above them were dark skies and bright stars. Descending from the clouds, she saw the faces of Jesus and Moses. As Moses moved back, a giant star of David superimposed itself on Jesus, and Jesus came close to Marie. The heavenly master told her that a time of fire and destruction would come, but she was not to be afraid. Until now, I had thought the story of the spiritual visitations and near-death experiences were fantastic, but I instantly knew that this story was the most important because it showed me what I believed was the purpose of all these previous experiences.

It is that Jesus wished us to know he was and is of the chosen people. He brought new love to the existing ancient theories about God's hope to expand religion into a creed that promoted the oneness of being and the belief in the one divine source. In that perception, all people were to be the chosen of God. As each religion finds common ground, they could eventually merge and, as one humanity under one God, coexist and live by God's loving law.

I kissed Anne goodbye and wished a blessing to this mother and daughter to know all was well. Only Anne's faith and trust in a Divine plan for her daughter would see her through the days ahead.

As I proceeded to my car, a gray dove flew over the hood of my car and landed in the grass before me. The bird and I sat facing each other in a moment of quiet reverence for those in Spirit who surrounded us with their love. They cooperated with me through the challenging physical life experiences I faced and taught me to call on God for help and for courage.

Listening to Your Inner Voice to Communicate the Voices of Spirit

When we are beginning any new endeavor, spiritual or otherwise, the temptation is to believe what the more experienced experts tell us. However, when developing your mediumship, it is critical to follow your own guidance, not that of other mediums. This was confirmed to me when I was asked to do a type of reading I had been cautioned against doing.

The moment I heard Karen's voice, I knew she was in distress. A few hours before, her daughter Jessica's boyfriend, Michael, had died in a horrific motorcycle accident. Karen, a client and devoted student of mine, had called me as soon as she received the tragic news.

I was so saddened for Karen, Jessica, and of course, Michael's family. Karen and I had become quite close over the past few years; she had traveled with me to San Francisco and Puerto Vallarta at a moment's notice and at great personal sacrifice. Indeed, her dedication to learning and honoring her soul's need to evolve was of a level I had rarely encountered, even among the metaphysical community.

Karen's daughter Jessica was a lovely person and very supportive of her mother's journey. A petite, sensitive platinum blonde, Jessica has always reminded me of Tinkerbelle, my favorite *Peter Pan* character. She moves with the same lightness of being. One morning, months before this unexpected turn of events, she had dragged herself out of bed at sunrise to drive Karen and me to the airport for our trip. As we left her car in a rush to catch our flight, I saw in Jessica's bright blue eyes a passing concern, perhaps a worry that we would not be all right.

Now those eyes were filled with the agony of loss, and my heart broke for her. She and Michael had been talking about marriage. Now, instead of planning a wedding, Michael's family was planning his funeral.

Despite Karen's belief in my mediumship work, I was a bit taken aback when she asked me to do a reading the very next day. I told her I would do my best, but that I had never done a reading so close to a soul's passing, when everyone's grief was so raw and fresh. Jessica might have difficulty hearing messages from Michael's spirit so soon after his death.

Other mediums have suggested that it is prudent to wait to do a reading until the deceased person's loved ones have passed through the confusion, anger, fear, and disbelief that make up the initial stages of grief. Many also believe that a newly departed soul is in transition and therefore often unable to send messages back to the earthly plane. I, however, do not usually follow restrictions given to me by any other medium, because I don't believe Spirit would ask me to do something that is not in the best interest of the person seeking answers. At the same time, I feel that Spirit will bring forth whatever is needed in the moment.

As I thought about the upcoming reading, I remembered a documentary I had seen on Lily Dale, New York. Lily Dale is an internationally known community of mediums and healers; it is also a place where metaphysical leaders come to lecture on a vast range of spiritual topics. One of the mediums in the film had reiterated what I had heard before: that newly departed souls are not capable of delivering messages, as they need time to acclimate to life in a higher energy field without a body. When I heard this, I doubted its veracity and was dismayed that the woman did not preface this by saying it was only her experience.

From the time I was a little girl, I have never restricted myself from exploring my own potential, as I know from my heart that I will either succeed on the first attempt or I will try again. I have always known that it is possible for us to do anything that is called for in the moment, if we listen to ourselves and not the criticisms or limitations of others. It was with this sense of knowing that I approached the reading for Jessica.

As soon as I got off the phone with Karen, I immediately went to my office and began a meditation, hoping to connect to Michael's energy. For the next hour, I received images and sensory perceptions from the young man, beginning with the sensation of extreme heat pulsating throughout my entire body. It felt like an embrace, accompanied by a tingling at my root and sacral chakras. What I was feeling was an almost overwhelming wave of love Michael had for his life, his parents, and for Jessica. His feelings for Jessica had all the beauty and purity of first love.

And Jessica had the same feelings for him that Juliet expressed about Romeo in William Shakespeare's *Romeo and Juliet*:

> *"When he shall die, take him and cut him out in little stars and*
> *he will make the face of heaven so fine that all the world will be*
> *in love with night and pay no worship to the garish sun."*

Soon I received an image of Michael showing me his memory of the accident. I sensed that he was catapulted over the handlebars of his motorcycle, much like an athlete in the pole vault event, who lifts himself high into the air, twisting and turning up over the bar. But while the athlete falls into a pit of soft foam mats, Michael's plunge was met by hard pavement. He hit headfirst and died quickly, without any awareness of physical pain. I then sensed the concern of passersby, followed by the professionals who responded to the 911 calls. They were carefully cushioning Michael's head with tenderness and respect.

I suddenly remembered how years ago, I had been driving along a major roadway close to my home when I saw a young boy get hit by a car and fly through the air, the same way Michael had. Unaware at that time that I was a medium, I had simply prayed for that young life. Now, as I read Michael, I wondered whether I had seen the soul of that young boy as he left the Earth plane.

Michael had so wanted to stay and live out his physical life. After leaving his body, he had looked over his shoulder, deeply aware that his mother, father, and Jessica would be devastated by this loss. But the souls above and ahead were calling him, and their irresistible beauty lifted him up. Despite his sadness for those he was leaving behind, he knew it was his time to go.

Several more images quickly flooded my mind, and I was truly amazed at the clarity of the images and communication from such a "young" man. Michael had been only nineteen years old, yet the expressions and feelings he relayed to me seemed representative of a more mature person. I saw the likeness of Air Force wings in my inner mind, or perhaps, it was the insignia of a police officer. Maybe, I thought, someone was interested in flying or lived near an airport.

Next, I sensed someone at a beauty salon. The person's hair was being washed and wrapped in a towel. I figured this was a reference to Jessica, who I knew worked at a salon. I felt strongly that a woman—either Jessica or Michael's mother—was feeling extreme anxiety. I knew that they would both need help in dealing with his death. Michael knew it too, and he gently touched my shoulders to let me know he would help them understand that he is still nearby. He would see them have success, joy, and move forward with as little sadness as was possible.

I had the distinct impression that people would be putting away his things or giving them to others. That is how it should be, as he let me know that his belongings were of no importance to him. He already knew in those early moments of being in Spirit that the eternal energy of his love could be shared by all who knew him, and that was all he wished to leave behind. They should—and would—find solace in his memory.

I sensed Michael working or living in a warm, bright outdoor setting, some rural place. This may have been his dream while he was alive, and I felt that it would be realized on the Other Side. Michael then showed me what his funeral would be like. I saw an altar server holding a cross, as well as a cross of flowers that some friend or relative had sent to show their respects. As I viewed the scene, I knew that Michael would approve of the service. Throughout the reading, I sensed there was peace for this young man and that he understood in Spirit what he had not been able to see when he was on the Earth plane. He knew that while he and Jessica were both too young to fully commit to one another, he was certain of his love for her. He regretted being jealous and trying to control their relationship by forbidding her to date others and not allowing her to have other experiences in order to learn more about herself. It was hard for him to put his insecurities aside, as it often is for all of us. He felt free now. Michael said, "Do not be sad. Think of me lifting up like a whale or dolphin coming from under the water and leaping into the sky, feeling the freedom of newfound power and joy at reaching for a higher sky."

I sensed he would help Jessica move forward so that she would have the good things she was supposed to have in this incarnation. He wanted her to release him, his physical being, but to remember the spirit of the youthful love they shared. His love for Jessica would always be there, whenever she thought of him.

Although these impressions were incredibly strong, I did not know at the time what each image represented. I just wanted to collect as much pertinent and physical information for Jessica and Michael's family, so I stayed in meditation as long as I physically could. As I met with Michael's loved ones in the days and weeks to come, they would validate each image, confirming that they knew now Michael had indeed reached out to bring them peace and comfort. Michael was also helping me to expand my gifts as a medium.

First, Jessica came for her reading. When I told her all I had seen, she was extremely moved. Through her tears, she said that it sounded like Michael was speaking directly to her. The messages validated numerous incidents that already happened and those that would take place at his funeral, which was planned at a local church a few days later. While she was so young to experience such tragic loss, she knew in her heart that the course of events following his passing was as it should be. Michael would not want her to hold on to grief, bitterness, and anger, as it would not be healthy for her. This was confirmed for her when Michael predicted that she would have a happy life and would know a different kind of love.

When I mentioned my impression of Michael in a rural setting, she said he had spent a lot of time in Upstate New York and that he wished to live there someday. He had also wanted to be a police officer and was preparing to train at the police academy; this explained the insignia I had seen.

Days after the service, Karen told me that Michael's mother gave away some of his sporting jerseys to his friends. Michael had been an altar server, and the priest he had worked with as a young boy gave the service. There also was a cross of flowers across his coffin. She also told me that he had always loved to see and hear planes passing over him, and had been buried by an airport.

A month later, I met Michael's parents. His mother had been delighted to hear that Michael had mentioned dolphins. Over the years, he had given his mother dolphin statues, jewelry, and pictures because the dolphin represented movement, beauty, intelligence, and moving through life freely. This was an important, profound message to help his mother remember that although he had left his physical body, her beautiful son was not only alive, but thriving and surrounded by other loving souls.

I even received clarification about the vision I'd had of the person having his hair washed at the beauty salon. Some months after Michael's death, I was hosting a psychic development group for my students. I asked Karen how Jessica was doing, and we started talking about all Michael had told me during the reading. Karen told me that when Jessica found out Michael had died, a young man named Adam, who was getting a haircut at the beauty salon where she worked, started to cry and put his arms around her. Jessica did not know that Adam was the brother of another of my students, Tara. Adam, as a sensitive, compassionate person, was put there to help Jessica through that very painful moment. I believe Adam was in the right spot, guided by Spirit to assist her. Nothing is random. We are helped through the most painful and challenging life experiences by our guides and ancestors in Spirit, who guide not only us, but the people all around us here in the physical world.

I was happy to hear that Jessica and Karen maintained their relationship with Michael's parents, even after Jessica began attending nursing school in Texas. As she spent the next two years growing in her awareness and gratitude, she was able to show Michael in Spirit that she would not waste her time in mourning and sadness. Instead she chose to live a life in service to others and make her family and Michael's family proud of her. After graduating from nursing school, she returned to New York and took a job at a special pediatric program, where she helps premature babies get past their difficult beginnings. Her compassion, persistence, and trust in life's preciousness are a testament to Michael's continuing guidance and love from the Other Side.

Contrary to what I had heard from other mediums, Michael—within hours of his passing—was able to come through for Jessica and his parents, providing facts of his physical life and a new vision of his spiritual life. This proved to me what I had always suspected: that I must trust that Spirit, not other mediums, will let me know the appropriate time and place to do a reading.

Since that incredible experience, I have on occasion been asked to do a reading for other newly departed souls. Like Michael, they too have given me messages expressing the love and appreciation for those they have left behind, while still expressing the connections of love, which remain unbroken by death.

Before the reading for Jessica, there was another man who had called to see if I could connect with his twenty-four-year-old son, who had recently passed. I told him I would do whatever I could to help, yet I was a bit anxious. The death was so recent and the pain and anguish of the family was overwhelming. I still questioned whether the impressions I would receive in the reading would show this father that his son was all right. If only Spirit would offer a seed of love that would speak clearly to the father's heart, helping him find acceptance for the accident that had taken his child from him.

As always, I went into meditation before my client arrived. Immediately, I sensed that there were three people in shadows in a boat, which was surrounded by a vibrant orange color. Then I sensed someone moving quickly, like agile loggers jumping from one log to the next. I felt that the young man who had passed liked dancing and to move fast. He also loved the nightlife. I then sensed a birthday cake with three candles, and I started crying. Someone would soon have a birthday.

The father of this young man appeared at the doorway to my office exactly at the appointed time. During the session, the father clarified all the impressions I received. There were three men in the car the night his son had passed, and they were by the water. The orange light surrounding this young man was his passion for dancing at clubs, and he had a dance routine using orange lights. Also, his football jersey was orange.

I felt this young man loved life and participated in his activities with enthusiasm and joy. He was well liked. I told the father to have a birthday cake with three candles for his son, as his birthday was coming up soon. He asked, "Why three candles?"

"Well, you have three children."

"No," he responded. "I only have two now."

I told him that he still had three children, but his son was away, still learning, evolving, and watching the people he loved on the Earth plane. I told him how my son Gregg was in California, and while I couldn't see him or talk to him all the time, he was still with me always. It was not all that different, I explained, with those in Spirit. Our loved ones are just in another room, and while walls may separate us, there is a doorway that will eventually bring us together again. In the meantime, there are also windows, which allow us to communicate with them.

I received other messages from this young man's spirit and gave them one by one to his father. Remember, all the medium has to do is provide the information as the person on the other side provides it. Often, a Spirit who wants to communicate with a family member gives a medium a message that can only be understood by the loved one in Spirit and the relative. This is proof to the person receiving the message that such communication is authentic. It helps to lighten the heart of those who have suffered a loss of their loved one. While validating messages might give some comfort, I also am acutely aware that no matter how much information a medium provides, painful thoughts and fears could return, and it might be some time before a parent can achieve some level of healing.

It is our nature to doubt what we cannot see or feel. This young man's father could not see or feel his son. As I was born with the sensitivity to receive these moving impressions from the energy of souls, I have no doubt about the survival of his son beyond this Earth plane. Often, the messages appear to sound and present like a foreign language. The messages need to be deciphered. I know I might misinterpret some of the clues if I put my personal spin on the idea, so I have been trained to accurately describe exactly what I feel, see, or hear in thought form and no more. What appears like a seemingly insignificant detail to me could be immensely meaningful for my client; therefore, it is important that I relay it to the client "as is." This is critically important when you do readings for others: simplicity is best. You are only the messenger, the conduit for Spirit.

At the end of the session, my sense of uneasiness was gone. I had done my best and I trusted that Spirit would continue to do the best for this suffering father. I would try not to fear any session after this, no matter how difficult the circumstances, as Spirit had once again confirmed that it only arranges what the client and medium are ready to deal with.

Just days after that reading, I met a young woman named Elsie. Originally from Mexico, Elsie mentioned that her brother Jesus died there when he was eighteen years old. Her mom always felt him around the house. When Elsie's mom talks about her children, she always says she has four children, even though only three are living. It reminded me that was exactly what I had told the man who had lost his son. Continuing to have a birthday cake on the birthdays of those passed over might offer joy and gratitude to help the connection to loved ones on Earth.

∞

"All of life is energy and we are transmitting every moment."
—Oprah Winfrey
The Oprah Winfrey Show Finale, Oprah.com

Loved ones are never lost, but are still interconnected to us by energetic threads from the heart, allowing us to feel their wisdom and guiding us to discover new paths to happiness on the Earth plane.

This week at my unfoldment group, several mediums gave me messages. It seemed my dad was present playing his violin. It wasn't a love song, but it was every bit as lovely. My husband David's father, in Spirit, said he was enjoying golf and playing as much as he wanted. David's uncle Tommy came through and he said that at his country house, being closer to nature, he was able to find God. I thought it odd that three men came through with messages for me.

A few days later, Caroline, who works with me at the office, called and said her father had a massive stroke. She asked me if I could do a meditation and find out what would be the best approach to handle this situation. She said, "You know life and death, and if you could let us know what my father's wishes are, I would appreciate it. He is on life support."

At about the same time Caroline called, two of my regular clients canceled, and I was immediately able to spend time meditating to retrieve helpful awareness of Caroline's father's situation. I then called Caroline and gave her several impressions I had sensed. I told Caroline her father was already on his journey to the next dimension and was not afraid. He actually was quite excited about the tunnel of green to the outdoors that his energy moved toward.

Caroline said the place I was experiencing was Ireland, as he so loved his remembrance of his homeland. All the messages were specific enough for Caroline and her family to know that they could not hold Jack on the earth plane any longer. He was ready to cross, but promised to meet them in a place they all loved to be together. That place was the old swing in the beach area behind Jack's house. I had seen that place he shared with his granddaughter Joanna in my reading. I offered to go to the hospital and to share Reiki energy with Jack.

A few days later Caroline called me and asked me to meet her in the ICU. I did, and while sitting next to Jack in his room, I asked his guides to help determine what Jack needed done. Immediately I had an impression of a wine bottle opener and a small helicopter. In the previous reading I had done in my office, Jack had implied he would take a rocket to his future destination beyond this physical dimension. I laughed because now he said to the family to enjoy his passing with a good glass of wine, and he would not be as far away as he had thought. He would only be a short helicopter ride away. With the messages from the men in my own family the night before, I realized that after this life, we might pursue activities we've loved while we are here on the Earth plane. Whatever and whoever is dearest to you will be waiting for you over there.

Our loved ones in Spirit can even help us by sending us messages about items that we have lost. I was reminded of this when my husband, David, and I were about to travel to California to visit our new grandson, Sullivan. Right before we left, David told me he had lost his wedding ring. We looked all over, but it was nowhere to be found. He was quite upset about it, and years before, I would have felt the same way. By this time, however, I understood that such an event happens just the way it is supposed to. I had become slow to anger, worry, or fear, and I had learned to accept loss as a necessary way to find something greater. I silently sent out the thought to Spirit, asking to find the ring. After we had arrived in California, David had an "epiphany"—or higher thought—from above. He called home and had Margie check his car, where she found the ring in the cup holder. He had put it there for safekeeping before playing golf.

Shortly after returning to New York, I was at the office when Kelly, a young mother of three, told me she lost her engagement ring. I told her about David's ring and how Spirit had guided him to remember where it was. I then asked if her ring was insured, and she told me it was. While we don't like to lose things, sometimes a loss gives us a greater appreciation of what we already have and helps us detach from the material world so we can see the larger world beyond the physical. The lost item may not seem as important as before. I told her I thought and hoped she would find the ring and that she was to tell me when it happened. A few days later, Kelly climbed up to the second steps of my office and announced joyously that she had found the ring. It was in her bedroom, where it had rolled under the bed.

Are these just two stories of rings lost? Actually, they were stories of what could be found when we had true faith and allowed help from a higher dimension. Trust and faith in ourselves and in those who support us, both here on the Earth and from above, are always available. *We need only ask.*

Expanding Your Gifts as a Medium

Like many mediums, it is not so easy for me to get impressions for people close to me. For the most part, however, I have been able to receive messages for anyone I attempt to do a reading for. My ability has developed greatly since I met the psychics from Lily Dale. During the course of a workshop conference with them, the five mediums from Lily Dale suggested that the energy and vibration of all the people present would be greatly enhanced as a result of the combination of the talents of those in the room and also by those in Spirit who assist us. Since that workshop, I am able to receive messages and information without having the person present for a reading.

Here are some things to consider when working on expanding your gifts as a medium:

We are unique.

According to Dr. Charlotte Tomaino, neurosurgeon and author of *Awakening the Brain,* each person's brain is unique, with different capacities for navigating the physical and spiritual dimensions of energy.

We have many kinds of intelligence.

All spiritual teachers, intuitive healers, and enlightened scientists recognize that there are multiple types of intelligence. They know that each person has a different life plan and that we all learn acceptance, patience, and empathy in our own way and in our own time. According to this concept, academic skills are only a small part of what we need to succeed in life. Just as there is visual intelligence and mathematical, linguistic, and athletic skills, there is spiritual awareness. We must respect the fact that each individual is free to develop whatever areas of interest and talents they have been born with. This new knowledge of the brain, being offered by neuropsychologists, is much like the concept of the Oneness University in India, which talks about the Oneness Blessing, or Deeksha, as the way to grace and spiritual evolution.

We need compassion for others.

There is a Buddhist prayer that states, "May all beings know love and kindness." It is a request for a peaceful and stable environment from the time one is an infant, as well as for the awareness that compassion is the key to living in a state of peace. This nonjudgmental compassion for others is also essential for anyone seeking to expand their spiritual gifts and connect with friends, loved ones, and guides on the Other Side.

We all take different paths.

It is also important to recognize the rapid global changes. Many people are actively seeking a state of grace as a source of personal power and a stimulus for growth on both the individual and collective levels. It doesn't matter whether you interpret synchronistic events ("coincidences") as answers to an intention or adhere to religious traditions; the important thing is to realize that it all comes from the Divine Source and to remain nonjudgmental of the paths of others.

We have many spiritual guides.

We all can walk in the world of Spirit and at the same time have a foot touching the ground of this world. This can be done by recognizing the gifts and blessings of life itself and your life in particular. All great masters—St. Francis of Assisi, Jesus, Moses, the Buddha, and others—have learned to quiet the drives and cravings of the physical body long enough to free the mind. In doing so, they were able to awaken to inner peace and to messages being given to them from Spirit. Through this connection, they learned how to improve the quality of their daily lives, as well as how to engage others with empathy, love, compassion, and kindness. I am aware we have many guides during the course of our Earth life, but I believe that each of us has three master guides that stay with us for the entire journey. Necessary guides and specialists in their respective field come in to help each of us as we tackle new challenges. The success of any challenge requires us to embrace the difficulty and breathe in the courage and whispers from the loving guides who support, honor, respect, and trust us. Remember to know or acknowledge them and return the energy of love. Is there a particular historical figure that somehow resonates with you?

Awaken to your spirit.

The world has vastly changed since the days when I first realized my spiritual gifts. Information on everything from meditation practices to holistic healing energy work is at our fingertips, bringing like-minded people closer together, regardless of geographical distance or cultural divide. These people are joining organizations, taking courses, and otherwise engaging in activities to break through their imagined limitations and live life as the spiritual beings they are. So feel free to engage yourself and others in any and all activities that awaken your mind's potential, challenge your physical body and open your heart and soul to your Divine purpose. Do not allow yourself to procrastinate or limit your exposure to new things: jump in the water and begin to swim!

Go beyond past fears and doubts.

Dr. Tomaino also discusses Theory U and an Open Heart, which guides us to recognize the emotional state and the presence of fear, sadness, loss, or any other emotion that holds us in the past. By getting past reluctance, cynicism, and fear, we can come to feel the truth of the present moment. The key to understanding where you have come from as spiritual energy and where you will arrive is only possible by recognizing the resistance in your emotions and the doubt in your thinking. It is by this action that you can learn to change the emotional state you are in to create a better you. When we do this, our soul energy falls in line with our physical life choices and manifests a new approach to whatever it is we wish to create.

Open your heart.

Spiritual evolution requires us to let go of past disappointments and reopen our hearts and minds to the truth of who we are. We must accept ourselves with all our talents and limitations and then recognize what people or events can assist us in getting past any restriction. In other words, who or what is it that will make your heart sing?

4

∞

Healing Hands:
Becoming a
Reiki Master Teacher

*If I want to share Reiki (spiritual energy) with someone, then I
would have to first re-discover spiritual energy within myself.*

—Frans Steine, International House of Reiki

You may be a person who has recognized that you have healing
abilities. Perhaps your hands are getting hot and tingly or you
intuitively know what is ailing someone else. Now what do you do to
develop this gift? There are so many different types of energy work,
and many healers proclaim that their modality is the "best" one.
Although I am a practicing Reiki Master and teacher, I disagree with
this view. All energy work comes from the same Divine Source, and
whether one is the healer or the client, he or she must choose the
method that resonates with them.

From the beginning, my Reiki practice has been guided by Spirit.
Like everything else in life, I only needed to open myself up to the
possibility and before I knew it, Spirit was leaving a trail of breadcrumbs for me to follow. If you are in doubt about how to develop
your own healing gift, ask Spirit and you will be guided to the
modality and people that are right for you. Spirit will also lead the
right clients to your doorstep, but you must truly be open to following the guidance and wisdom you are downloading, even if you may
have questions about how events are unfolding. In other words, ask

questions when necessary or even when in doubt, but stick with the plan of LISTENING. This was probably the most important commitment I made to Spirit, and myself when I began this journey.

I signed up for a three-day retreat that my mentor, Robert Brown, was hosting in the Bahamas. In the days before I left, fifteen new clients made appointments for energy healing which, of course, pleased me to no end. It was as if Spirit was confirming that I was on the right path, especially since I originally had planned to leave for the Bahamas several days earlier. "Coincidentally" my plans had changed, which made me available to treat these new people.

Expanding the Gift of Energy Healing

Spirit also guides those who are seeking healing to arrive at my door, even if they are unaware of it. In fact, they may not even "believe" in energy healing, at least on a conscious level. They make an appointment because their shoulder hurts or they get tension headaches, but there is much more to it than that. Unlike traditional or Western medicine, energy healing is not simply a physical experience, but an ancient, powerful force that clears the stale or negative energy we have collected during our earthly lives or even before this lifetime. The energy worker begins to move this energy, which eventually facilitates a physical or emotional healing.

Other people *are* aware that energy work is partially a spiritual practice and avoid it because they are afraid it will alter their belief systems. It's important for the practitioner to explain prior to a session that Spirit is guiding them. Indeed most of my clients are acutely aware that the energy is of a higher nature and not in conflict with any belief system. Since nothing is random, my roster of clients is divinely selected. If I had gone on the trip to the Bahamas several days earlier, as originally planned, I would not have had sessions with this group of clients.

Filled with quiet anticipation, at last I reached the Bahamas. The weather was perfect, warm, but not humid, and the surroundings were quiet and peaceful. The event was being held at the Xanadu

Hotel, where Howard Hughes spent his last years. It seemed a fitting place for a spiritual conference, considering many people still claimed they could feel his presence there.

I had attended Robert Brown's events before, and I immediately noticed that the group was much larger than the previous year. It was a collection of mediums and other spiritually-minded people interested in broadening their awareness of psychic and spiritual phenomena as well as those bereaved by the loss of a loved one. I recognized several who, like me, had attended these conferences before, but one woman immediately caught my eye. She was wearing a beautiful crystal necklace with a six-sided pendant. It reminded me of something that Barbara, a woman in my healing group back in New York, had told me in a reading. When I was on my trip, she said, I would find a crystal with six sides.

That afternoon, I went to the little shops along the shoreline, looking for a six-sided crystal. The first two stores did not carry them, but when I asked the saleswoman in the third store, she smiled, nodded, and took out a clear white crystal. It was her last one. I noticed that, in addition to the six sides, it had a clear spot that resembled a doorway. As I stared at it, I became aware that the doorway was a message. Spirit was telling me that I would develop more clarity and discernment in the information I received from higher energy. Perhaps the crystal necklace would help me with my meditation practice. I also knew I could use it to help show people the movement of their own energy centers.

For example, if one holds a pendulum over the energy center of a body, and the pendulum does not move, it means that chakra is closed and needs healing work to help it relax, rebalance, and reopen. Each chakra is associated with specific health issues and different life situations relating to family, work, and spiritual or soul development (I discuss these energy centers—or chakras—further in chapter 6). I relate this story now, however, to demonstrate how Spirit had lead me to the crystal that would assist me in my energy work.

Other mediums have also guided and informed my own spiritual transformation so that I am better able to serve my clients. Some-

time after the trip with Robert Brown, I attended a workshop hosted by Dr. Carmen Harra, an accomplished psychic medium and psychologist. Her approach is centered on the belief that it is impossible for us to go forward without resolving old problems and patterns of behavior. She therefore helps her clients understand themselves and their life purposes by focusing on past karmas and resolving past life mistakes.

Dr. Harra had written a book called *Everyday Karma,* which had
been endorsed by Deepak Chopra. As she addressed the crowd, I
remembered a seminar I attended where Deepak Chopra had spoken. His energy, as well as his words, were so profound that it had
taken all my focus and concentration to absorb the material. It was
the same way for me with Carmen and I did not want to miss a word.
Both Carmen and Deepak's teachings went far beyond being psychic; they interacted with higher intelligence in a way that was
dynamic. There was no question that they have the same life purpose: helping humanity evolve to a higher plane of love and connection, both to God and each other.

Carmen's message resonated deeply with me, as I also feel that
humanity is on the precipice of the next step in evolution and that
many will be attuned in this new Age of Aquarius. For the next two
thousand years, I believe we will be on a journey of personal self-
actualization of our souls. This will bring the world to a unified
understanding of divine energy or God. Carmen was talking about
numerology and codes and our individualized life plans. In my first
book, *Life Is No Coincidence,* I also referred to these codes and our
personalized life plan and destiny. In addition, I referred to the
signs and messages that we received through coincidences and synchronicities in our daily experiences.

When Carmen opened the floor to questions, I raised my hand.
She immediately told me that the book I had written was missing a
piece of the puzzle, and she offered to help me find it. I had not
even mentioned that I was finishing a book. She said that she saw
the book cover with my picture on it and light emanating all
around. Carmen also said that the publishing of the book was not

as far off as I thought. Next, she said I had three guides around me. One of them strongly wanted this project to be realized. Later, when I purchased Dr. Harra's book, she gave me a card and told me to call her.

After reading my book, Carmen told me that it reflected the beauty of my discovery—namely, that life on the Earth plane appears to be an illusion, separating us from our true soul life. When we reconnect with the Divine energy of our being and the God source, we are then free to do the work necessary for empowering and expanding our soul energy. As each soul's energy emanates from a dimension of eternal life, by making the connection between our subconscious and conscious mind, we can eventually become whole and heal, avoiding needless suffering. At that time, when the evolved soul leaves this life, it can choose whether it wishes to have another physical life in the visible world or remain in the invisible dimension.

I have found that as I work to expand my understanding of energy and myself, Spirit bequeaths new spiritual gifts and skills that I may incorporate into my work. It has become clear to me that the more I work with the healing energies surrounding me, the more defined my abilities and work become. Constant effort is the only means to developing your personal power. A new ability I became aware of is being able to read the energy of a person *before* they visit me for an appointment. Even if they are far, far away, when I meditate and mention the person's name, impressions and an understanding of that person's situation become clear to me. This understanding assists me in helping them not only on a physical level, but on a spiritual one, and that is how energy healing works. You don't have to be a medium *per se* in order to be a force for healing, and yet all energy healers should develop and use their internal guidance system or intuition when working with clients.

For example, one of my Reiki clients recently missed her appointment. I wasn't worried, as I instinctively knew she was okay. I had already done the meditation for her, during which I envisioned her pulling the sheet over her head. There was a wave, almost like a drawing of a watery wave, coming over her and her husband. I thought it was a reference to a cruise they might want to take. Then, I saw a colorful Venetian mask. When I spoke with the client later, she explained that she often slept with a covering over her head. She also told me that her husband wanted to go on a trip to Venice, Italy, where they made those masks. Instead, they had opted for a trip to the Venetian Hotel in Las Vegas and had a great time.

I responded that her mother was showing her the balance in her marriage and to accept that it is not possible to appreciate any experience without having the opposite experience. Then my client said her mother always told her to be happy, and that her husband was as good as gold. With these few impressions, she knew her deceased mother was still close. She was watching over the family and giving her encouragement. My client was comforted, and seemed to have a greater appreciation for her marriage. Spiritual messages can reinforce what is special and good in our lives even if it is not perfect, and this helps our bodies heal as well as our souls.

Discovering the Many Methods of Energy Healing

While my practice centers mainly on Usui Shiki Ryoho, a Japanese Reiki healing system, I have also studied several other healing modalities, all of which have aided my spiritual growth as well as that of my clients. The central message at these seminars has been that all healing methods work with the God Source energy within us. Many teachers and mediums told me that there are healing energies—angels, loved ones, or ancestors—present in our environment. All energy healing treatments tap into a person's natural ability to receive and realign their energies to these and other universal healing sources.

This was further confirmed during my recent trip to San Francisco, where I attended a class with Australian teacher Ruth Rendely. Ruth works with an energy healing system called *Seraphim Blueprint*. The flight seemed longer than usual, but that may be because I was impatient to get to the training. As always, I was excited to learn a new tool that would assist me in aligning my clients' energy. I was not disappointed. During the meditation attunements and instruction, I felt the tremendous energy present in the room. It flowed through my body, leaving me no doubt of its potency to clear the body of blocks and stale energy.

I have also been guided to study with Dr. Eric Pearl of *The Reconnection* and Laurie Grant of the *Arch Energy Hawaiian Healing*. These systems are dynamic and powerful, and I encourage each person to choose what serves them best in their own healing and growth processes in an effort to merge alternative healing modalities with Western traditional medicine.

In my observation, each healing modality offers great benefits; one is not better than the next. Combinations of wellness and preventative therapies offer people the best approach to staying healthy and vital. We are drawn to certain experiences, people, practitioners, or treatment plans by guidance from a higher force, as they know what will best suit our individualized needs. As we receive the whispers from above, it is our choice to listen and respond, or not. But if we chose to listen and respond, we will discover that a program that incorporates several healing techniques, such as Reiki, craniosacral therapy, reconnection, chiropractic, massage, reflexology, and a host of others will help everyone protect their physical and emotional well-being. Prevention first, followed by healing and maintenance next, are the keys to a life of holistic health. It was one such whisper from above that led me to study reflexology.

I had a reading with a medium who sensed the presence of my father, Myron. In life he had been a podiatrist, and now he was telling the medium that he thought I should study reflexology. Reflexology is a scientific approach based on the principle that by stimulating reflex points on the feet or hands that correspond to organ and body parts, homeostasis or greater balance can be brought to the body. Foot reflexology required a great deal of technical knowledge about the physical, structural, and hormonal functions of the body. It is a primarily preventive approach, but in the right circumstances, can expedite the healing of illness and injuries. Following the clues and assignments as promptly as given to me by Spirit, I registered for a reflexology workshop where I met several interesting people, including a few other Reiki Masters. In addition to learning another healing modality, I had found yet another precious group of like-minded friends.

My father came through with another message, this time at my unfoldment group. One of the other members said I should go back to the place I had received a message from my father the year before, for there was another message waiting for me there. So I went back to Lords Valley, Pennsylvania. While there, a woman asked for a healing session. She had sciatica and had been unable to get to her chiropractor. I told her it would be my pleasure to offer her this.

During the session, I received an impression of a female associated with the art deco period or style. My client told me that her aunt had just given her an art deco ring that had belonged to her mother. She felt that the ring was really a gift from her mom in spirit. She also felt her mother's presence in the room during the session, which seemed to be a confirmation that the ring had indeed come from her. I gave her another impression, this time of the large, black face of a terrier. The woman replied that such a dog had been seated in her chiropractor's car the day before, but more importantly, she also had a dog in spirit that looked exactly like what I described. I told her that by showing itself to me as a big face, her dog in spirit was letting her know he wanted to be thought of as more important than the dog she had played with the other day. The funny, loving, playful dog didn't want to be forgotten!

My friend said her hip felt much better and she wanted to give me a gift for the healing work, as it could only be appreciated and respected if paid for.

The next day, we had lunch at a lovely, quaint teahouse. There were small accessories for sale there as well. My client picked up a small, old box and said, "I want to give this to you."

When I first looked at it, I didn't find it all that attractive. Upon further inspection, however, I noticed a blonde angel. One of her hands was giving the "thumbs-up" while the other was holding a small box with the word "Candy" written on it. When I opened the box, I found a chocolate candy kiss. I knew this was the message I was supposed to find. I often brought candy kisses to my office, and my dad had always given a thumbs-up sign to show acceptance and approval. I don't believe I would have seen this small angel box if my friend hadn't given it to me. It now sits on a shelf in my office. It is a gift from a grateful friend and a message from my dad in spirit, who loves the work I am doing.

As I mentioned earlier, my process often feels like following the breadcrumbs. You may also find that your journey to finding and developing your intuitive healing and medium abilities is a slow one. The truth for developing and refining our souls is often buried under years of denial, fears, and misunderstandings. For each of us, true awareness about the depths of our being is often a slow unraveling of debris and misconceived beliefs. It takes much courage and fortitude to dig deep into the heart of our spiritual foundation. It also takes patience and a refusal to give up, even when things feel uncomfortable. Discomfort is normal as you expand to new levels of awareness.

One of my Reiki Master teachers, Barbara, is advanced in her channeling techniques and has other spiritual gifts, which she has been aware of since childhood. I have been involved in all these pursuits only for these past eleven years. I am trying to do everything to follow the path and to catch up for lost time. However, I can only progress as fast as is humanly and spiritually possible. My guides may know the time frame, but I do not.

We all must learn to accept Spirit's timing. At the beginning of establishing my Reiki practice, I had six devoted clients who I felt would benefit from learning to practice Reiki. One in particular, Barbara Flaherty, had been waiting for me to teach her. In fact, she continually reminded me of it. I explained to Barbara that according to a recent reading given to me, it would happen eventually. Barbara agreed to wait for me.

Experiences of Healing in My Reiki Practice and as a Medium

Finally, the time had come to teach my first Reiki class. Of course, Barbara Flaherty was there, as was Barbara, one of my Reiki teachers, and a third Barbara, who was part of the class. The Barbara who was assisting me asked the class to close their eyes and listen to her read a poem that expressed the true healing intentions of Reiki. As I watched the women, I was so proud to have been able to have them all together in true connection. A feeling of love and joy filled me. I was doing what Spirit had intended, which was to bring worthy and receptive initiates to the beautiful Reiki path, one of giving to others through receiving the Divine light and healing energy around us. *This continuous flow of love and proactive energy could heal people on emotional, spiritual, and physical levels.*

One day, during a stroll on the boardwalk, I met a woman who told me she was a practicing real-estate agent and was thinking of changing careers at this point in her life. She was fifty-one years old and thought it might be too late in the game to find a new career. I told her that acclaimed architect Frank Lloyd Wright had achieved most of his success after his seventieth birthday and had, in fact, been productive well into his nineties. We continued to chat for a while and she asked for my business card. When she saw my office address, she mentioned that she was a patient of Dr. Bass, a previous owner and chiropractor in that building. When she had started seeing him she was in so much pain she couldn't even get out of bed. Dr. Bass had come to her house four days in a row. Over the next twenty years, he had not only treated her using chiropractic treatments, he also shared ways she could improve her life, including exercise, stress reduction management, and nutritional changes.

Like many chiropractors, my own included, Dr. Bass was committed to helping his clients achieve and maintain holistic health of the mind, body, and spirit. They understand that medical practitioners can set up an environment for change, but cannot heal anyone. Each individual must make their way forward experiencing greater gratitude, love for life, and for change. This is the blueprint that can bring us to a healthier place.

Walking with this woman was her friend, Sheryl, who heard us talking. She mentioned that she had a friend, Sabrina, only forty-two years old, who was battling pancreatic cancer and asked if I could go to her home for a session. I told her I would go to her house if she were unable to come to my office. I had done that several times in the past and was thinking of how Dr. Bass had also done that for a patient who needed it. That afternoon, Sabrina called and arranged an appointment. A few days later I met Sabrina, a petite, pretty, young woman with bright blue eyes.

We were immediately comfortable with each other and talked at length. Sabrina told me that right after the appointment had been made, she was in the car seated next to her husband who was driving, and something made her turn. Sabrina quickly noticed my name written on the professional billboard they had passed and smiled at the validating coincidence. During the Reiki session, Sabrina let me know she felt intense heat and pain in the area behind the pancreas where the cancerous tumor had been removed. She also felt heat to the front of her stomach. During any energy healing session, in order to restore a troubled area to balance, pain or other sensations might be vaguely noticed and are only short-lived. At the conclusion of the hour-long session, Sabrina was relaxed and smiling and scheduled her next appointment. I instructed her to practice the relaxation-breathing exercises I had shown her.

Sabrina remarked that she had an extraordinary surgeon, who had the foresight and skill to perform a surgery that two other doctors had not approved. Sabrina would've died within six months without this surgery. She felt that God had put him there to help her, and now felt I was put there to help her restore her strength. Sabrina admitted to having fears and control issues, but wanted to continue Reiki sessions so she could learn to go beyond any stifling emotion that might be hurting her. She even asked if it would be possible to study Reiki, and asked if it would help her have greater faith and bolster her courage. She wished to know if Reiki could help alleviate fears and help her to accept her health issues as a means for good and not a punishment. I confirmed that Reiki was ideally a tool for conquering fears and building stronger emotional fiber and also a stepping-stone to a higher view of possibilities.

Within a short time, Sabrina did accept her illness as her way to create a stronger bond to those she loved. She realized that her survival and health relied on her ability to think positive, healing thoughts, to release negative beliefs, and to incorporate new behaviors and actions moving her past untamed emotions and responses—the anger, greed, judgment, and blame, which may have contributed to her illness.

A positive thought process definitely could improve the quality of one's day and also the possibility to improve any situation. Correcting any mistake in our actions or behaviors does not guarantee defeating any disease or challenge in our life. It will always be good for our soul to experience a better way to act rather than react. However, we each come with a life plan and a time to depart our physical life, but while here must use every opportunity to reveal the best from within ourselves. I only hoped to support and encourage Sabrina's daily treatments, helping her draw on her own inner strength. She needed to disperse any negative and fearful thoughts that quite possibly contributed to the stressful conditions that created the cancer in the first place. Perhaps, having cancer was the path by which her soul would fight back and grow to a higher consciousness. Sabrina undoubtedly would find her life path improved through more trust in herself and God. It might be possible to use the illness to fuel the spark of spirit in her heart. Sabrina expressed to me that she had hope that with God's help, miracles could be created.

All the impressions and messages that I received for Sabrina showed her that I had knowledge of certain life events for her even though I had never met her before. She knew the messages were there to relieve her fears and encourage her to continue to fight her way back to her life.

At the same time I made these home visits to Sabrina, a young woman I met over a year ago while having dinner with my husband at a local restaurant, called for a session. She told me that since we had talked a year ago, she had made changes in her life and felt ready to go forward and leave her emotional debris behind. At the time we met we had discussed energy healing. She was very interested in what we had discussed and had held onto my card all this time until she was able to schedule an appointment.

That evening I told David what a wonderful session we had shared, and that I believed her life would continue to improve. Her openness and positive thought processes would make that possible. I realized that often a person is unable to pursue a spiritual encounter until they are ready.

Another woman who had been speaking to me for over two years woke up one morning and made an appointment. Did a whisper from someone in spirit encourage her? Why had it taken so long for her to contact me? The impressions I receive from spiritual sources for my clients are intent on awakening them to a higher level of functioning on the physical and spiritual levels of their lives. The information in the readings seems to me to be close to 100 percent accurate, and they serve to determine the focus of the major issues that are worked on during the second part, which is the hands-on healing.

While the messages usually do not give specific directions for how to proceed, for they allow for a person's sense of free will and personal choice, the messages do offer clarity in understanding present or past events. To me, they seem like a report card from upstairs showing love and acceptance, never judgment or reprisal, in the same way a good teacher motivates and assesses their student's progress.

Some mediums feel that energy healing and readings need to be kept separate. A British medium at Robert Brown's retreat had said to the group that they are two distinct energies. I am not sure why she was so adamant on the subject. My gift combines both. The messages from the loved ones' spirits that I receive both before and during sessions help with healing or clarifying thoughts and with improving the physical and emotional body.

For example, with one client, I physically felt intense and extreme coldness going to the lower back and the woman told me she had had back surgery some time ago for a herniated disc. Healing was still going on in that area. With another client, I felt pain and numbness in the left foot, and suggested she arrange a visit to a podiatrist where a cyst was found that was pressing on the nerve and removed before causing any damage.

Another woman was feeling dizziness and having headaches. I felt a disturbance in her thought patterns and she announced that the neediness of the people in her workplace was stifling her own spiritual growth. I suggested she ask for in quiet prayer or meditation her wish to be in a workplace with people who she could find more common ground with. The universe might just provide an opportunity if it was in her best interests. However, sometimes it's not the place or people making us uncomfortable, but our own perception of the situation. When we change our thinking, we change our reality and then anything is possible. By focusing on what you need for your own happiness, you may create it.

I visited Sabrina again and received pleasant messages from Sabrina's father in spirit. Each beautiful message and remembrance of their time together helped her feel connected to his love and gave her some relief from her fears and worries. Her father was an important influence in her life. Sabrina was an only child and her attachment to both parents was unusually strong. On this particular day, when I arrived at her house, she told me she had called my office to reschedule. I had never received that information. As it turned out, we did sit down to share a cup of coffee. I gave her some of the messages that I had received prior to visiting her.

All of a sudden, she told me the most remarkable coincidence. If I had not gone that day, I would never have heard this amazing story of Sabrina's miracle. Sabrina explained: "Two years ago, my daughter Jennifer was in a serious car accident. She had bleeding on the brain, two collapsed lungs, a lacerated liver and spleen, and they had to reconnect a severed arm. The doctor told my husband and me to get her affairs in order. Jennifer's life hung in the balance."

The doctor would've loved to tell Sabrina a likelihood of a fairy tale ending, but it didn't look good. Sabrina walked to her car, praying to St. Jude, the saint of impossible causes, and said, "Please let it be me and let me lay down in her place, for if you take her I will have to kill myself, and I don't want to kill myself."

That same night was May 21, Jennifer's birthday. Jennifer awoke and asked what time it was. Sabrina looked at the clock. It read 1:40 a.m. Sabrina said to Jennifer, "It's your birthday and thank God you are here with us on your birthday." When Sabrina went home and checked Jennifer's birth certificate, she discovered that Jennifer was born at 1:40 a.m. Sabrina knew God had given her daughter a second chance at life.

Three months after her daughter's recovery, Sabrina was diagnosed with cancer.

At her request, Sabrina received her Reiki level 1 attunement in her home. I asked my former teacher Barbara to support me in my efforts and to help Sabrina on her road to wellness. I have found that sometimes when you combine the energies of several loving healers, there are stronger possibilities for success. For some reason, I never doubted that Sabrina would recover and be well. Other mediums in my group were not as confident as I was. Regardless of the outcome, I knew Sabrina's Reiki training was helping her deal with the side effects of her chemotherapy treatments and to remain calm and hopeful.

It is my personal feeling that a medium should never predict the client's death, even if they believe they sense that possibility during the reading. Ultimately, the time of passing is holy and only decided by a higher power. Changes in the plan of life and death can be altered by circumstances.

I was with a client who had just arrived, and while we were talking, my cell phone rang. It was Sabrina's husband, who said that Sabrina was in Long Island Jewish Hospital. She had developed a blood clot after a bout with the flu. Sabrina had continued bravely to wage a war battling cancer. I completed the session with my client and proceeded to the hospital.

When I arrived at the hospital, Sabrina had her CD player on with the music that I had given to her for her Reiki sessions. There was a small, soft, stuffed giraffe to keep her company. We all need our comforts and toys, especially when we are ill. Sabrina's friend was just leaving. Sabrina told me all that had happened over the last few days. She asked me to conduct a healing session on her. Then her son, Anthony, who said he had heard of me, walked into the room. I had not met him before. He wished to have a session also.

I was telling Sabrina some of the impressions that I had received for her. First, I saw two people putting their heads together in a loving way, actually touching their foreheads together. I felt someone's wrist bothering him or her. Sabrina wasn't aware of what it meant, but Anthony knew exactly what I was envisioning and said that he always put his forehead lovingly to his wife in an expression of oneness. Anthony's wrist was actually hurting him. It would seem to me that touch, sharing thoughts with love, might help heal wounds and hurts. Spirit obviously knew that Anthony would be in the room, and the message would show him the validity of a medium's ability to perceive happenings not only for a client, but also for their loved ones.

Sabrina's husband arrived and graciously thanked me for my concern and help. He said, "There are things one cannot understand, but that doesn't mean it doesn't have validity or substance." I asked Sabrina to remember to use her Reiki skills to help her relax. I hoped that Reiki would sustain her in the quiet moments of the night in her hospital room by helping her know she would not be alone.

Later, as I looked through the many items in the hospital gift shop, I came across a small box. On the lid were a sun, moon, and stars on a blue background; inside was a small star. It reminded me of the lyrics I had heard during a reading a few days before: *"Catch a falling star and put it in your pocket, never let it fade away."* The song reminded me to give up my worry and to have continued faith in our life plan and the help that would always come to us from Spirit.

5

∞

Not Your
Mother's Doctor:
The Growing
Acceptance of
Energy Healing

Healing ... is not a science, but the intuitive art of wooing nature.

—W. H. Auden
"The Art of Healing"
Collected Poems

This line, like so much of Auden's poetry, captures an essential truth about life, love, and what it means to be human. The human body is hardwired to heal itself, a fact that, until recently, was largely ignored by Western medicine. Not too long ago, if you told someone, particularly an MD, that you were an energy healer, they would have laughed you out of the room. If you happened to be one of the few open-minded doctors and expressed these views to your colleagues, you'd be laughed right out of the hospital. Now, decades after W. H. Auden penned the poem "The Art of Healing" and dedicated it to his personal physician, the medical community is finally catching up to him.

The concept of what constitutes good health practices is continually evolving. It used to mean having a checkup with your MD. If he or she said everything was okay, it was okay. If your doctor found

81

illness, you took a pill, were scheduled for surgery, and so forth. These days, however, health is not just about the physical body. Technological advancements have brought wonderful things to our world; they have also meant less exercise for our bodies and more stress for the mind. Our need to be constantly "plugged in" to our computers and smart phones has resulted in sensory overload that can distract us from our true nature as Divine beings. Perhaps that's why mainstream magazines, websites, and blogs now include methods for meditation, yoga, breathing exercises, and relaxation practices for the body and mind. The same is true of energy healing, which the National Institutes of Health now lists as a branch of complementary and alternative medicine being given an unprecedented acceptance in Western culture. Even some of the most traditional doctors and nurses now acknowledge that alternative health practices are a vital piece of the holistic puzzle.

The Increasing Practice of Energy Healing in Western Medicine

I am always overjoyed to hear members of the medical community embracing energy work as a way to heal pain, clear negative thoughts, and align ourselves with Spirit. I have had the opportunity to interview many of the leaders in the medical community on my radio show, *Healing from Within*. In fact, I have noticed over the past few years that an increasing number of my guests are doctors, surgeons, psychiatrists, and psychologists who combine their traditional medical training with intuitive and/or energetic healing abilities.

Recently, one of the people at my office who had not been fully aware of the benefits of Reiki walked over to me and said, "You are ahead of your time. I just saw an article on the amazing results Reiki can offer." Only the week before I had read an article in *The New York Times* about a doctor with an internal medical practice who was recommending Reiki for depression and other health issues. This doctor, as well as other doctors, was becoming aware that alternative healing modalities offered a more moderate approach for treating many conditions and could often yield satisfying results, sometimes avoiding the need to order medications for their patients. Dentists and doctors alike were also using Reiki sessions prior to surgery to help patients relax and deal with pre-surgery jitters. Reiki could also enable the healing process to take less time and lighten the painful effects of surgery.

Later in the afternoon as I returned home from a reflexology course I was enrolled in, I was standing on the Long Island Rail Road platform bound for eastern Long Island. Standing next to me was a young, attractive black-haired woman, friendly and talkative, like me. Her voice and mannerisms caught my attention and reminded me of somebody, but I couldn't quite make the connection in the moment. I focused on what the young woman was saying. All of a sudden, I realized that she sounded just like my cousin Adria. While Adria was resistant to my spiritual stories and reality, this young woman was more open to the possibilities. She mentioned that her internist, Dr. Susan Groh, was a Reiki Master. As Da Vinci's Vitruvian Man is a representation of the mind, body, and spirit connection, it is my hope that the new crop of health professionals like Dr. Groh will use their educational training along with their intuitive insights for greater healing of their patients by offering a more balanced and proficient way to practice medicine.

A few days later, the other woman I had met at the reflexology workshop called me. I told her the story of the young woman I had met on the train. She said that she also lived in Queens now, but still traveled to see her doctor, Dr. Susan Groh, in Merrick, Long Island. Then the young woman said, "Now I understand what you were telling me about all your coincidences. You do seem to have more than anyone else."

A few weeks later, I was scheduled to host a demonstration of energy healing at the Bristol Assisted Living Center in New York. Barbara, one of my Reiki teachers, agreed to assist me as I was expecting a large group. I hoped each resident could experience the hands-on healing energy of Reiki. I was thrilled to see filled seats in the gym and exercise area. After introducing Barbara and myself, I opened the discussion with an important question, which I knew the senior citizens might have had excellent answers for. The question I asked was, "What do you believe helps to contribute to a long, productive healthy life?" The answers were numerous, but it became obvious that all the seniors present were curious, anxious to learn, and motivated to have new experiences. They all appeared to have positive attitudes. The one answer they hadn't given in response to my question was the need to seek alternative health practices for continued vitality and health.

During the introduction, I had explained the history and the benefits of Reiki. But talk was only talk, and people need to experience the feeling of a healing touch. I turned on some soft music and led the group into a quiet relaxing meditation. Barbara and I proceeded to every person in the room, allowing the peaceful energy that flowed through us to transfer to them. Most of the people seemed happy with the experience. They asked for leaflets and cards to tell other people about the experience. I was grateful to have the opportunity to share Reiki with so many new people, some of whom would undoubtedly spread the word to others.

Choosing a Modality of Energy Healing

There are several types of energy healing. Some, like Reiki and acupuncture, have been around for thousands of years; others have been developed more recently. Their methods may differ, as well as certain aspect of their ideologies, but they all operate on one basic premise: there is more to us than our physical bodies. Energy sessions focus instead on the life force—or "qi"—that flows within all living things, the goal being to release, dissolve, or transmute negative feelings that block this force and cause imbalance and illness in the body. All of these methods have benefits that range from improving or healing the physical body to clearing past painful memories and negative thought patterns.

Acupuncture

This is undoubtedly the most well-known form of energy healing. It is also one of the oldest. The acupuncturists inserts needles along the meridians (or energy pathways) of the body. In Chinese medicine, these meridians are believed to affect every system and organ of the body. In the United States, acupuncture is most often used for pain management. In its truest form, however, it is all about the release of energy blockages. A close relation of acupuncture is acupressure, the only difference being that instead of needles, the healer presses on these certain areas of the meridians to remove blocks and promote the free flow of qi.

Chakra Tuning

This practice is a form of sound healing that is used to balance the chakras, or energy centers, in the body. It is believed that each chakra responds to a particular frequency, which can be used to tune it and promote physical, spiritual, and mental wellness. Sometimes the healer will use tuning forks, set to these frequencies, to restore the energy flow. Another way to tune the chakras is through mantras. Each chakra is associated with a specific primordial sound, and when chanted, these sounds help to keep the chakra open and balanced.

Reiki

This ancient Japanese technique is used to relieve stress, calm the mind, and promote balance and healing within the body. While one does not have to have any particular belief system to practice or receive Reiki, its use can be traced to the Bible and has been used by religious healers for centuries. It is literally the "laying on of hands." In fact, some people believe that Jesus was using Reiki when he healed people. The word itself is the combination of two Japanese words: *rei*, which means, "God's wisdom" or "the higher power," and *ki*, which is "life force energy."

During a Reiki session, the healer's hands transfer universal energy to the patient, who in turn heals him or herself. This energy flows to any areas of the body where it is needed the most and rebalances the person's *ki* to restore health and well-being. For those people already in good health, Reiki is an excellent preventative measure for continued good health. It has many benefits, including muscle relaxation and pain relief. It also aids in digestion, stabilizes blood pressure and blood sugar, and strengthens the immune system. Sometimes it completely heals the condition. Even when the disease has seemingly progressed too far for recovery, or in a hospice situation, Reiki can create a peaceful state, relieve physical symptoms temporarily, and reduce stress.

Of all the energy healing modalities, at present Reiki has probably received the most attention from the mainstream medical community. In fact, several US hospitals now employ Reiki practitioners. According to a September 2012 article in USA Today, "A research study performed at Hartford Hospital in Hartford, Connecticut concludes Reiki treatments have improved patient sleep by 86 percent, reduced pain by 78 percent, reduced nausea by 80 percent, and reduced anxiety during pregnancy by 94 percent. 75% of the patients who participated in the study also said that they would 'definitely want service again.'"*

The Seraphim Blueprint

This modality is based on the work of a group of high angels called the Seraphim. It is believed that thousands of years ago, these angels came together to assist in the evolution of humanity, and that they even guided the early Hebrews in the creation of the Kabbalah. The modern healing version of this ancient technique was developed in 1994 by Ruth Rendely, a meditation instructor, after she was visited by one of the original Seraphim. In the previous chapter, I discussed the powerful training I absorbed when I attended a workshop with Ruth in San Francisco and for a year listened to teleconference workshops with Ruth originating from Australia. The Seraphim Blueprint is essentially a collection of eleven major ener-

---

* William Lee Rand. "Reiki in Hospitals," www.reiki.org/reikinews/reiki_in_hospitals.html, accessed September 30, 2013.

gies that work with our life force energy to harmonize our nervous system and promote physical and emotional well-being. While they work in concert, each of these major energies has its own special purpose and quality that moves the person toward self-realization.

Quantum Touch

This relatively new method following in the path of the ancient Reiki healing art is based on the premise that we can harness the power of our own love to heal those around us. It has also been found to be an excellent tool for pain management, reduction, and even elimination. It also has been known to heal disease, balance organs and glands, and even heal burns and injuries.

Like the other modalities, it works with a client's own life force energy to promote health and healing on several levels. The practitioner is trained in ways of focusing, amplifying, and directing this energy to the areas that need it. Those who teach Quantum Touch claim that it is so easy even young children can learn to practice it.

Distance Healing

All of the above modalities can be used, not only in person, but in another state or town—even another country. This may be difficult for our three-dimensional human minds to comprehend, particularly when we are just beginning our practice. In those moments of doubt, we must remember that Spirit knows no limitations. I, too, once found it hard to believe that Reiki could help someone thousands of miles away, but an incredible experience involving my own son convinced me, once and for all, that Spirit is bound by nothing, not even geography!

When I picked up the phone and heard Gregg's voice, I thought he was calling to see how our trip to Alaska was. David and I had just returned that day. Instead, I was horrified to learn that two doctors had discovered a painful growth under his armpit and he had been scheduled for a biopsy. Beside myself, I wanted to fly out to California to be there for him, but Gregg assured me that he would not be alone; his friend Tim was going with him to the hospital. When I spoke to Barbara, my Reiki Master Teacher and a medical intuitive, she said she sensed a dark mass in Gregg's armpit. She told me I should be there for the diagnosis. My stomach in knots, I asked my healing group if they would be so kind as to assist me and send distant healing.

A week before the biopsy, my Reiki group met. I set the intention to send distance healing to the time, place, and people involved in the procedure, especially Gregg. Then, using an ancient Reiki symbol for distant healing, we all summoned up all the thoughts, intentions, and love for a successful outcome to this procedure. It was scheduled on September 16, which is my birthday and was the first night of Rosh Hashanah that year.

On that day, I was in the office waiting for a new client. All the other doctors and practitioners had left the office already to celebrate the holiday with their families. I would have been out of the office also, but had received a call from a client who needed an immediate appointment. She had originally scheduled a session five months before and was unable to keep the appointment, but despite that—and my own plans—I did not hesitate.

While I waited for her, a little boy who I had spoken to many times walked in for his occupational therapy session. He usually came in with his mother, but this time his father had accompanied him. I introduced myself, and my heart leapt with joy when the father told me his name was Timothy. Whenever I have met a person named Timothy in burdensome times in my life, *Timothys* have offered spiritual help, a sense of peace, and an immediate sense of hope. This is a sign for me to know that Spirit is sending me a message that everything will be all right. Like any mother, I was still terribly worried about Gregg's procedure, but meeting Timothy reminded me again that Spirit was there supporting Gregg and that it would all work out for the best.

After a while, my client showed up and we had a wonderful session. "Sheryl," she said before leaving the office, "you have helped me beyond my wildest hopes."

I returned home, happy that I had kept the appointment and brought relief to the young woman. As I got ready for my dinner plans, Gregg was never far from my thoughts. I looked at my watch and saw it was exactly the time that the procedure was to be performed—three o'clock New York time, twelve o'clock California time. I bowed my head, and put my healing hand under my armpit. While using the ancient Reiki symbol, I prayed to Spirit, saying that if my son was all right, I would thank God every day for the rest of my life and be of service in anyway directed. I suddenly felt something burst or explode in my armpit, and then felt a warm green healing gel spread over the whole area. As a new Reiki practitioner, I had no idea what was going on.

Immediately after that experience, I jumped in the car with my husband and a guest, and headed out for dinner at my sister's home. While driving, my cell phone rang. My husband answered the phone and it was Gregg. Gregg reported that the procedure was over and the doctor had just returned and told him that there was nothing to send out to pathology; only scar tissue remained, and he was okay.

I started to cry and thanked God from within for what I knew was a true miracle, and proof of the healing power of Reiki.

Since that first distant healing experience, I have been called on many times to use Reiki: to help a new mother recover from the pain of a caesarian delivery, to assist a young man recover from a stroke, and to help people in hospice situations transcend their fears and look ahead to new life. Whether a simple medical procedure or more complicated health or life experience, Reiki may help to bring peace and calm to quiet the fear of all those involved while supporting the soul's needs at that moment.

Dealing with Spiritual Doubt

There is no spiritual person—past, present, or future—who has not had to overcome doubt. Even the Ascended Masters had moments of disconnection from the Source, so the rest of us surely will. To think otherwise is unrealistic and self-defeating. Like everything else, doubt is just another life lesson and we are in control of our reaction to it. You will also find that when you are faced with some-one's doubt about your spiritual gifts, you are actually facing *self-doubt*. This is what you really confront.

One evening, I was at the office, waiting for my unfoldment group to begin. Brian Katz, a chiropractor who shares the space, walked by and said, "Sheryl, what are you still doing here?"

"I'm waiting for my people," I remarked absently.

Brian laughed. "Your *people*? Are you Moses now?"

It zinged me for a moment and I thought about giving him a sar-castic response. Then I realized he was just making a joke. It was I who was in doubt about the connection I had so often felt with Moses. I paused for a moment, then looked up at Brian and smiled. "Right."

My group arrived and I quickly forgot the incident. Later, my for-mer Reiki teacher Barbara told me that during a meditation she saw Moses standing behind me. He was saying that I was like him—I thought I wasn't able to do what Spirit needed me to do, just as he had not believed himself to be a great leader. He said that, like him, I would have the help I needed to complete my mission. Moses had brought freedom to his people. I too seek to free people, not only from physical bondage, but from the fears of the ego so they can know their eternal essence. I realized that Brian's offhand comment had forced me to look at my own self-doubt and allowed the mes-sage from Moses to come through.

Dealing with Practical Concerns

One day, I had lunch with a young woman from my reflexology class. She had soulful, soft brown eyes and was about the same age as my daughter Stacey. The woman had some minor health issues that caused her to seek alternative health modalities. She also was aware of her own spiritual path, and from an early age was aware of her intuitive abilities. She knew that her spiritual friends found it hard to earn a living in their chosen paths. In the past, I had had many business involvements, had worked full time, and had success. Having a successful husband allowed me the luxury at this stage of my life to study, practice Reiki, and write full time. I was not making a lot of money, and knew that it would have been exceedingly difficult to support myself.

So, I told other young enthusiasts of spiritual pursuits to secure their financial well-being through conventional work experiences while following their spiritual goals as a hobby. Some heeded this advice, while others were so committed that it was not an option to retreat from the challenges of a spiritually-guided life. Whatever your choice, just make sure you are following your inner guidance rather than a misguided notion that to be spiritual you must forego money. Sometimes we must deal with practical concerns while pursuing our spiritual path; it is all part of the journey.

The Role of the Energy Healer

As these modalities are further integrated into our healthcare system, we will undoubtedly see more and more people pursuing energy healing as full-time careers. It is important for all to understand their role in the healing process. The healing itself is an agreement between God and the patient's soul. The healer—whether he or she is a Reiki practitioner, MD, or both—is merely the conduit of these healing energies. In addition, the patient can also learn to directly connect with the healing energies, particularly through meditation.

Marisol had come to me for a reading and healing session. For some time she had been experiencing pain that her doctor was unable to diagnose. During the hands-on healing part of the session, I sensed a blockage around the second chakra (lower abdomen) and Marisol confirmed that the pain was in this area. She had had a gallbladder operation, and I sensed an imbalance of energy in that area and felt a thickening of scar tissue. After the session, she thanked me and said she would return for another session soon. When I didn't hear from her, however, I didn't question it, for I learned long ago that things will unfold as they are supposed to.

A year later, out of the blue, I received a call from Marisol. After thanking me for my help and apologizing for being unable to return, she told me that in the four months after our session her condition had continued to worsen. It had gotten so bad, in fact, that she had been unable to function in her daily life. She had visited several other doctors, none of whom was able to pinpoint the cause or offer suggestions for the relief of the pain. One day, during meditation, she sensed or heard, "Sheryl said it was scar tissue." She returned to her doctor, telling him that scar tissue from her previous surgery may be the cause of all her suffering. Acknowledging that this was possible, the doctor sent Marisol for physical therapy, which included myofascial release therapy. It was the successful method to deal with her pain!

Marisol asked me for a meditation or prayerful reading that she might use for her continued healing. I wrote the following *Meditation of the Sea and Sun* to help her and all who have pain and wish to connect to that higher dimension:

- Begin by sitting in a quiet place where you feel safe and will not be interrupted.
- Soft, gentle, background music always helps to quiet the mind and find a connection from one's soul energy. It helps us go to beyond this time and place, where healers and loved ones in Spirit are always by our side but unable to be recognized, until we do the work and allow ourselves time to feel these energetic connections.
- Next, use a visualization process, which may be activated by reading or with eyes closed; simply remember the content of this meditation.
- Imagine yourself grounded to the earth, with threads from your feet seeking the core and life force of this planet.
- Breathe up this energy throughout your body, feeling each cell energized and filled with green, healing, life-force energy. Bring energy from above and create a spiraling channel of light within.
- Now imagine you are on a boardwalk and there are seven steps to bring you to the warm sand or Earth. Count from one to seven,

feeling yourself becoming more relaxed as you move slowly to the bottom.

- Feel the ground below as you walk towards the body of water—it can be the ocean, a lake, pond, or river.

- Look up at the sun, feeling the warmth and brilliance on your skin; and closing your eyes, feel this warmth deep within, spreading to all cells and healing all cells of your physical and spiritual Being.

- Feel yourself as a light being connected to all of life's energies and each loving aspect of yourself and others.

- Imagine a person you know or remember that fills you with Divine love and joy. Feel your heart open to a selfless way of love and being.

- Once filled with this love, see yourself within the cool splashes of a magnificent, full, flowing waterfall at a fantastic place you have visited or seen in a picture. This water flows over you and through you. The cooling effects make you feel fresh, renewed, and in alignment to beauty, peace, and purity.

- Think of loved ones in Spirit: a relative, a religious figure, a higher vibrational being who joins you. Ask this soul to show you the beauty of fire, water, air, and earth, as these elements are the forces of our eternal life flow. **ASK** to be guided to what is needed for your expansion, health, prosperity, and greater sense of love and compassion.

- In this state of gentle vibration, relaxation, and connection **ASK** for what you need to heal—an emotional concern or a physical pain.

- **ASK** to be brought forward, away from limited thinking and to become the expression and radiance of the divine light of your essence. This will allow situations and people more in tune with your higher interests. A state of healing is created as a result of these intentions and actions, leading you to living with hope, faith, and wellness.

- **See** and **feel** a release from within your deepest cellular structure and know that by requesting to release any negative thoughts or toxins in the body, it will happen.

- Know you are loved and connected to the Universal Source of Life where love, peace, and health are the normal state of Being.

- Thank yourself and those in Spirit who are present for taking the time to be in this silent, loving place of Unity and Oneness.

- Remember you are a divine spiritual being having a glorious physical life.

- Always express your intentions in your own unique way, as in this state of silence and connection to the divine you will always be downloading what is right for you.

- Allow yourself the grace to co-create multidimensional healing for yourself and others.

- SEE, FEEL, AND HEAR THE CLOSENESS OF THE DIVINE: THE BEAUTY OF LIFE WITHIN YOU AND AROUND YOU. Be grateful and be the essence of Love conquering fear and moments of doubt.

- When you open your eyes, feel CALM. SMILE and bring that state of well-being with you throughout the day or night. Share your good will and best actions with everyone.

- Hold your personal power, which is the gift of the soul expressing itself. From WITHIN, you will focus the brightest and lightness part of your creative self and you and the world will resonate in joy unbounded.

- These words and thoughts bring your guides and surrounding life support team closer to your inner knowing so you may feel safe, triumphant, and divine.

As indeed you are!

6

∞

Getting Your Own
Spiritual House
in Order

Let nothing disturb thee,
Nothing affright thee
All things are passing;
God never changeth.

—Saint Teresa of Avila
Hispanic Anthology: Poems Translated from the
Spanish by English and North American Poets

As in every other aspect of life, it is one thing to "talk the spiritual talk," and quite another to "walk the spiritual walk." When we begin to integrate the Divine into our human existence, we want to make sure we leave behind negativity, past hurts, and outdated ways of thinking that will impede our growth. This process is often full of joy and wonder; it can also be heartbreakingly painful. The important thing to remember is that the process, often lasting years or even an entire earthly lifetime, will be quite a ride. While reasonable minds can disagree as to whether "instant enlightenment" is possible, for most of us spiritual transformation is a gradual thing, marked by "aha" moments that motivate us to keep going. First we must discern what no longer serves us, and then we must figure out how we can let it all go.

For many of us discernment is the major problem. We enter this earthly incarnation with a particular set of circumstances, both positive and negative. They include things like our families, physical characteristics, personalities, talents, ailments—the list goes on and on. As we move through life, we internalize the belief systems of the physical world around us, so much so that it is often difficult to figure out where beliefs end and where we begin.

Understanding Our Emotional Landscape

One way to do this is to examine our emotions, particularly those we consider negative. While interviewing Dr. Richard Moss, author of *Inside-Out Healing: Transforming Your Life Thought the Power of Presence*, on my Internet radio show, he described "intelligent feelings" in contrast to our "untamed emotions," which are heightened reactions that lead to exaggerated responses. He suggested that if we attend to our "ordinary emotions" to evolve them into feelings that are intelligent, they can offer us great insight, and give us instructions about how to engage in our experience. But emotions that are corrupted by our ego remain "unintelligent" and often lead us into unpleasant associations and suffering.

The area of financial abundance is a good place to start because there is usually a clear connection between how we feel about our finances and how our parents felt about money when we were growing up. For example, do you feel like money is the "root of all evil"? If so, why do you feel this way? Did your father stress out over the bills each month? Did your mother think that it was impossible to be successful and close to God? If these beliefs are negatively impacting your life (i.e., making it difficult to manifest abundance), it is time to clear them. The same is true of any limiting beliefs you may have.

Everyone, whether they realize it or not, has picked up and internalized someone's beliefs or emotions at one time or another. Feeling any unbalanced energy affects all people to varying degrees. However, intuitives, mediums, and sensitive people learn not to "take on the weight of the world." People not familiar with energy protective mechanisms may internalize negative energy, walk around feeling bad, being the unwitting bearers of other people's baggage. It becomes possible by utilizing a clearer understanding of the laws of energy to move past other people's pained expressions and inappropriate behaviors while maintaining a light and hopeful outlook, that these people will hopefully find ways on their own to move past their emotional baggage.

One day I was leaving my yoga class when another student, Carol, asked for my business card. She told me she was someone who was known as an "empath," or someone who can "read" the thoughts and feelings of others. Empaths can see below the surface of a person's demeanor to sense what is really going on with them. A "side effect" of that ability is that the empath is often deeply affected by others' energy. They must find ways to protect themselves in order to maintain the integrity of their own vibration. Many empaths feel people's *physical* ailments. Dictionary.com defines an *empath* as someone who has the capacity for "the *intellectual* identification with or vicarious experiencing of the feelings, thoughts, or attitudes of another."

As an empath, I can relate to this. During a healing session, I can often locate the area where energy is disrupted by feeling pain or inflammation within my own body. I might also feel the client's anxiety, hunger, joy, despair, anger, and other emotional or physical sensations. At times, the sensations received do not belong to the physical energy of the client. These sensations could also be messages which belong to the energy from the client's loved ones in Spirit, who are validating their presence by sending recognizable signs, including but not limited to the manner in which they passed or from health conditions they had during their lives. At one session, for example, I felt a great pain in my head. I was reading Mike, who then told me his father had died from a head injury. Then, I felt a great heat, as if my entire body had burst into flames. I was sweating all over! When I told Mike what I was experiencing, he said his uncle had died in a fire and that he had just been thinking of him.

Realizing how I had learned to use my empathic qualities to sustain my personal sense of well-being and development, I was thrilled when Carol told me she wanted to come to my group meetings for healing practice and meditation. She also wanted to develop her psychic abilities and learn additional ways to energetically protect herself and effectively use her emphatic gift.

Over the years, I've met many people who have a great interest in developing their spiritual gifts. Yet often they do not pursue this path, either because of personal reservations or because they are afraid of how others will see them. To these people, I like to quote twentieth century writer and shaman, Lynn Andrews: "We must walk in balance on the earth—a foot in spirit and a foot in the physical."

Self-mastery is an ongoing process. We are changing second by second, and so is the world around us. We will never completely know ourselves, or anyone else, for that matter. What is important to realize is that we are not limited by our thoughts and dreams. We are not just beings of essence or spirit, nor are we merely physical bodies. We are both!

Once we learn to focus and concentrate our thoughts in a consistent manner, without doubt and negativity, many of our best intentions will come to fruition. I have observed and concluded for myself that happiness is not based in power, or in the accumulation of monetary goods and possessions. Rather, happiness is in the joy of giving and receiving and elevating oneself in the positive, eternal energy dance in this physical dimension and with awareness of our higher spirit.

When I first began following my spiritual path, and indeed everyone's path is a spiritual path, one of the first things I noticed was that all of my teachers—regardless of their other methods—always spoke of the need to raise our vibration in order to receive information from a spiritual dimension. I seriously had no idea how to raise my vibration. Did they mean I needed to use a hoola-hoop and continue to move my energy in circles? It took me a while to realize that for one to raise their vibration, he or she must eliminate negativity, selfishness, fear, and an overall attachment to the physical world.

A higher vibration means contemplating and practicing a higher love of self and others. We must, on a consistent basis, speak from the heart and soul, rather than from the ego or the mind. This brings us back to the issue of discerning what beliefs are ours and what we have picked up from others. There are many ways to learn what works for us. Quieting the mind through meditation, music, nature walks, dance and movement, sex, gardening, and enduring relationships will help us to do this.

Interacting with others who are interested in raising their own vibrations, using their God-given talents, and serving humanity is another excellent way to transform physical energy and merge with spiritual energy.

As you are able to quiet your mind and let go of needless chatter and self-doubt, you will eventually begin to sense your Higher Self, that part of you that is unconcerned with the minutia of everyday life. You will begin to know yourself experientially, rather than intellectually. Eventually, this quieting of the mind will allow you to receive information from other dimensions.

As an intuitive healer, I have discovered that when I meditate or allow my body and mind to let go of thoughts, and focus on the person coming for a session, I receive mental impressions, words, thoughts, songs, and even feelings such as pain, anxiety, joy, or love. All of these impressions reflect information about a client's life: past, present, and even future events. Some of the information comes from relatives and friends in Spirit who have passed from this physical plane. Their thoughts of the heart and mind, energetic in their nature, have passed from the physical body upon death and do remain viable in the atmosphere. By all scientific, as well as spiritual, accounts, energy cannot be destroyed, so the essence of a person's thoughts and soul continue beyond their physicality. This was confirmed by Dr. Eben Alexander, the well-known neurosurgeon and author of *Proof of Heaven: A Neurosurgeon's Journey into the Afterlife.* After his near-death experience he moved past skepticism and doubt to the realization that consciousness survives physical death.

Once we truly feel and listen to our spiritual companions having a physical life, and those companions beyond this earth plane who are still with us, the meaning of who we are often becomes clearer. We are physical beings, really four-dimensional, resonating and vibrating through our thoughts and creating the lives and situations around us. Through meditation and in the dream state, we can transcend this physical body and contact our eternal and true being. Each of us is connected to the cosmic forces of an ever-evolving universe, as we are ever-evolving souls.

Balancing the Energy of Our Mind and Heart

A young woman stopped at my office door and asked if I was the one who does Reiki healing. I responded that I was. She explained that she had had a Reiki treatment thirteen years before and that the healing power of touch had piqued her interest. She had gone on to become a massage therapist. She was also a licensed special education teacher, but had found over the years she was more interested in her spiritual growth. Her husband, on the other hand, remained more concerned with the day-to-day machinations of life. As a result they had grown apart, and she wasn't sure the marriage would survive. Clearly this young woman was at a crossroad in her life, and was very open about discussing it.

In addition to her marital troubles, she was trying to figure out how she could pursue her spiritual interests while continuing to work her regular job. With three children, she was not in a position to give up that income.

This story is all too common in today's fast-paced world. Most people find that they are only able to afford "part-time" spirituality. It is even more difficult when one person in the relationship wants to develop their spiritual gifts while the other is content to exist solely on the physical plane. This seems to be particularly true of women, who are still usually the primary caregivers. They often stretch themselves too thin as they take care of their spouses, children, and work responsibilities. This can present challenges to their spiritual work and be detrimental to their health and emotional well-being. We all need a support system, particularly those women who are working, raising a family, and trying to fulfill their own Divine potential. It helps if their partners remain open-minded and both parties learn more authentic and truthful ways to communicate and tune into each other's emotional needs. I think there is a greater shift toward these kinds of authentic relationships, but there is still much work to be done.

First and foremost, we must remember that we are all on different levels of understanding in regard to our true nature, as well as having a different approach about how to apply energetic laws for more successful living. When we do not utilize these laws effectively, we create friction with each other—even fallouts with those closest to us. It is only by striving to live in accordance with universal laws, respecting other's choices, and sharing this awareness that we can hope to connect to our higher selves.

Highly conscious human beings, now and in the future, are the templates for the evolution of humanity and for the creation of a finer state of harmony and balance. It will be in the sharing of our dynamic, beautiful, inspiring thoughts and in rethinking and reprogramming any limiting thoughts, that the shift will move many of us to a more productive level of purer thought and action. With great self-awareness and Cosmic awareness come a greater responsibility to share and exchange these ideas with those who will listen.

When a person becomes aware of existing energies, emotions, and the motivations for their behaviors, they then can finally understand how to balance their own energy. Remember, thoughts can be of the ego-mind, or they can be emotions and feelings from the heart or soul. They can also be memories of a soul's divine nature. Awareness of which aspect of our thinking is motivating us to action can help us make more conscious decisions. Observing and interacting with people who receive energy and messages intuitively from Spirit, and are able to balance the energies of mind and heart, are examples for us to learn how we may function at the highest level possible in a human state.

The Spiritual Wisdom of Children

Have you ever known a child that seems wise beyond his or her years? Know things they couldn't "possibly" know? We often call these children "old souls" when the truth is, all children are aware of Spirit, much more so than adults. We come into this three-dimensional world very aware of the paradise—and the friends—we have left in order to have a human experience. As we grow up, most of us learn to ignore these gifts in the face of "reality." However, in order to remember our true Divine nature and realize our spiritual gifts and, indeed, the gift of life, we must often disregard this physical reality and learn to see things as we did as children.

One day, I met the child of the future. I was in my office when suddenly a beautiful, dark-haired girl stood in my doorway. She had a sweet face with dimples and when she smiled her clear, bright eyes always looked directly into mine. They reflected a calm maturity beyond her years. Although she was only eight years old, this child who stood before me represented an evolved, sensitive, and spiritually awakened soul.

"I am Nicole," she said, "And my mom is coming to see you as soon as she is done with the doctor." She told me she was Greek and Turkish, and later I found out her mother—who was getting acupuncture down the hall—was from Columbia.

"Sometimes I have dreams," she continued, "and the things I dream happen."

She was sensitive, soft-spoken, and exuded an aura of grace, beauty, and power. I was rather in awe of her. I told her that most people are intuitive. She responded that she knew she was psychic and this sometimes scared her. I told her I was psychic also, and received impressions when I did energy healing on people, and such a gift helps us understand others and ourselves. The information we receive often improves our health and increases our knowledge of the world.

"Don't be afraid, Nicole. When you are grown up, you will use these skills and gifts and do great things in the world."

Prior to her mom's session with me, I received certain impressions from Spirit. There was a female angel, as well as a male energy in a triangle, that surrounded this child. During this session, her mother told me that they lived together with her brother. Her mother was a spiritual and religious person and so thankful for her extraordinary daughter.

I made a reference to Don Quixote, which she immediately attributed to her dead grandmother, who had been born in Spain. After the session that lasted an hour, the woman's child turned to me and said, "Thank you for helping my mother, and you and my mother will always sleep protected by Angels." Perhaps, she was aware of the angel that I had seen in the impression for her mother. I thought the remark so beautiful, loving, and sensitive, and I was grateful that God sent such a special gift to me in the form of that little child.

I believe as we evolve, all children will have these intuitive gifts and will use their awareness of love to improve the world community. In the meantime, however, we must learn to recapture our own childlike wonder if we want to remember our true nature as spiritual beings and fully offer our gifts to the world.

A new client, Tara, whose son Liam visited the office for occupational therapy, came for her first session. Before she arrived, I sat quietly and listened to a tape entitled *Divine Healing and Prosperity,* which was composed by Dr. Harold Grandstaff Moses. I often use this music for my healing sessions, since it quickly relaxes me, as well as my clients.

Some months before, I had been told that I must begin to get impressions before my client arrived for the appointment. On that day, as I sat quietly, I sensed two souls in spirit, two females, possibly a grandmother and aunt. There was a lot of golden energy around them, and I had the feeling of extreme love and support.

I always ask my new clients to set their intention for the healing session. Tara expressed her need to let go of stress and worry for her four-year-old son, Liam. Liam was a challenge—a lovable, autistic, and expansive ball of pure untamed energy. We began the session, and I immediately felt the energy or involvement of the grandmother and aunt in Spirit.

When I mentioned this to Tara, she said that before coming to my office she had prayed and asked her grandmother and aunt, whom she loved greatly, to show their support. Her wish and intention were simply and profoundly answered. Tara confirmed my other impressions during the session, except for one. Towards the end of our time together, I sensed enormous large black eyes and a volcano with orange fire spewing out of the eyes. It didn't mean anything to either Tara or me at the time, but I told her that sometimes the impressions make sense later.

Before leaving work that night, I saw a children's book called *The Castle in the Attic* lying on the floor. I picked it up and noticed the main character was a boy holding a miniature silver knight. His name was William, and that is the name of my deceased grandfather. My son, Gregg William, is named for him.

Observing and feeling the magic of this childhood tale reignited a memory of my own dreamy state of being when I was a teenager. Weeks ago at a reading, I was told to remember the dream I had when I was seventeen or eighteen years old. I did remember the dream. It was of Don Quixote, from the Broadway show *Man of La Mancha*. There was a song in that show called "The Impossible Dream." When I was younger, this song meant so much to me. Perhaps the words spoke to my soul. I even used it for my wedding song because the song expressed the need to struggle with love and life and to achieve what others might think impossible.

When my son was young, he used to say he would put me in the attic when I was older. Perhaps, he wanted me above him to watch over him, or being a sensitive, bright child, he was afraid of my dying. I just knew I had to read this book. It became apparent and clear to me there was synchronicity surrounding the story in this children's book and my own life.

The knight's name was Sir Simon. One of my teachers had expressed to the group that a guide of hers was named Simon. The best friend of William, the main character, was Jason. When my son was young, his best friend was Jason. The woman William loved in the story was Mrs. Phillips, an English nanny. My son had a nanny who had a strong influence in his development. Later in the story, Mrs. Phillips transforms into Lady Eleanor. I have an Aunt Eleanor. At the end of the book there was a guard, a protector named Brian, who helped William defeat the evil Wizard. I work with a colleague named Brian, who has helped me understand certain healing concepts.

It soon became apparent, however, that there was also in this children's story an important reference for Tara and Liam. In the storybook, William faced a black-eyed dragon while playing the song *The Battle Hymn of the Republic* on his musical recorder. William refused to back down, even when the dragon spewed flames in his direction; he just continued to play his recorder. William stood his ground. Within the reflection in the dragon's eyes, William could see his image replaced by an erupting volcano.

That was the impression I had seen and given to Tara earlier in the day. I felt the message reminded us that as long as we understand that fears are only illusions, and if we don't give in to our imaginary fears, nothing could harm us. It was in this moment of truth and without fear that William was able to slay the dragon. As William looked into the dragon's eyes for the last time, he saw a terrified and lonely cat imprisoned in the dragon's body. Once the dragon was destroyed, the cat was free to return to his loving mistress.

I was sure that the volcano referred to Liam, as his energy was also imprisoned within his body. The gifted, lovely, little boy trapped by the challenges of autism would be released from certain restrictions over time. I believe this message of conquering the dragon and releasing the imprisoned cat was a form of guidance from Spirit intended to help Tara and her family achieve success in dealing with Liam.

As I sat in meditation before Tara's next session, I sensed a dragonfly with two pairs of wings and enormous eyes. This dragonfly was climbing up from darkness into white clouds and golden sunshine. This was confirmation that Liam would grow and develop, despite his challenges, and so can we all, if we just remain committed to seeing the world with childlike wonder and innocence.

Some years ago, I discovered a book called *Animal Magic* by D. J. Conway that describes symbolism involving animals, as well as other ways in which we can understand the human personality and the relationship animal totems may serve in giving us further spiritual messages. This book has proven invaluable, and in conjunction with my readings, the information about the animal in the reading offers my clients a greater understanding of their life situations. After my meditation with Liam, I turned to the page that discussed the dragonfly.

The book described the dragonfly as one of the most beautiful of all insects, and one that represents swiftness, illusion, and change. One of the magical attributes of this insect was its ability to break down illusion in order to transform a person's life. According to some Native American legends, the dragonfly was once a dragon! This description, when added to what I had already read in the children's book, seemed to be a guided message to Tara on how to deal with Liam's forceful energy.

Balancing and Transforming Energy

In ancient societies, for instance in Greece, Rome, and North America, people always found ways to connect to the deep healing resources of the earth by grounding and drawing up the essential life force minerals, nutrients, and water content—all necessary components for our physical well-being. These societies followed spiritual practices to attain higher consciousness for combining the energy of the planet and the universe for sustaining a physical life. Physical health and emotional well-being reign supreme in a simple and holistic way of interacting with the physical world. Ancient cultures also used all forms of beautification of the physical body: elevated consciousness by exercise, meditation, art, theater, dance, and vibrational music. In other words, speaking to the soul through beauty and creativity, instead of the mundane, were ordinary practices for survival.

In addition to these methods, one can become aware of his or her personal energy and power through hands-on therapies such as Reiki, craniosacral, reflexology, acupuncture, massage, deep breathing techniques, or yoga. Meditation, prayer, or performing service to others is also instrumental for generating higher awareness. These activities can also help us transform and clear limiting or negative beliefs we have taken on from others.

The balancing of our chakras is essential to our physical, emotional, and spiritual well-being. Each energy chakra corresponds to certain areas of the body. These chakras are affected by life experiences or issues, and pain or illness in a specific chakra area often indicates negative energy or life practices that must be healed or transformed. In addition to the major chakras discussed below, there are ancillary chakras in the hands and feet that affect our ability to manifest and receive our spiritual gifts.

Root (first) Chakra

Located at the base of the spine, this chakra governs our sense of connectedness with the earth. When this chakra is opened and balanced, we feel supported in our earthly endeavors. When it is out of balance, it can manifest physically, as in lower back pain, and/or emotionally, such as in a fear of a lack of support.

Sacral (second) Chakra

Located within the lower abdomen, this chakra is the seat of our creative and sexual or sensory energy. When it is open and balanced, we feel comfortable expressing our sexuality; we also feel confident in expressing our creative talents, whether through drawing, writing, dancing, or other activities. When this chakra is blocked, we have difficulty experiencing pleasure and feel stifled in our artistic endeavors.

Solar (third) Plexus Chakra

Located just below the ribs, this chakra is where our true Divine selves reside. It also represents our personal power, and when it is balanced we feel comfortable in our own skin and feel confident in our abilities. We do not give our power to others, nor do we try to take their power; instead, we respect the integrity of all.

Heart (fourth) Chakra

 Located in the chest area, this chakra represents our ability to give and receive love. It is also the place where our desires for our lives are kept. When we live from the heart, we are attuned to our spiritual nature and know what actions to take for the highest good of ourselves and those around us. Our relationships are based on equality and mutual respect, and we are able to give freely without expecting anything in return. When the heart chakra is blocked, we tend to act from the ego, focusing more on the concerns of the physical world and cut off from Spirit and our own Divine natures.

Throat (fifth) Chakra

Located at the base of the throat, this is the seat of our communication system. When our throat chakra is open and balanced, we are in touch with our personal truth and feel comfortable communicating it to others. When this chakra is open, we can also access the guidance coming from our friends, loved ones, and guides from the Other Side. On the other hand, when this chakra is blocked, we have trouble finding our voice, or perhaps say things just to please others, even if it is not for our highest good. Physical problems include thyroid issues or anything involving the throat.

Third Eye (sixth) Chakra

Located in between the eyebrows, this chakra is part of our internal guidance system from Spirit. It also represents our ability to see spiritual reality.

Crown (seventh) Chakra

Located at the crown of the head, crown chakra represents our connection to the Divine. When it is open, we experience ourselves as aspects of God and co-creators of our lives. When it is closed, we may feel lost, alone, or trapped in this three-dimensional plane.

Energy healing, including Reiki, is an excellent tool to open and balance the chakras. This ancient, hands-on method relaxes the body so the person can connect to his or her energy flow for the purpose of finding balance, peace, harmony, and an understanding of their essence.

Reiki opens all energy channels in the body—including the chakras—for receiving and passing healing energies. It enlarges a person's capacity to develop intuitive gifts, which we all possess and for some even helps them to receive messages from Spirit. All of us are following these intuitive nudges and guidance from that higher spiritual arena of life often without being fully aware or awakened to this fact.

I believe we have come into this earthly incarnation so that we may experience the duality of this plane. It allows us to grow spirituality as we learn lessons from each new challenge and transcend the many problems of physical life. Only a true blending of the better aspects of love and Spirit will help us to love ourselves, our ego and physical being, as well as our souls.

Mediums help others understand that consciousness transcends death and something of that physical person survives, including all the experiences gathered while in a physical body. This freed soul, filled with new awareness and experiences from a physical life, is now still learning and expanding in the spiritual dimension beyond this Earth plane.

While on the Earth plane, however, mediums also provide service in helping people understand and grow into their spirituality. I have found that my spiritual messages for clients help them explore their life purposes and destinies, as well as fine-tune their physical, emotional, and spiritual components. With added information from spirit, we are able to go beyond just the awareness of life in its purely physical aspect and cope with any situation.

After all, life is about us using all of our senses to lift gently into an awareness allowing us to feel and understand energy and life beyond the physical world. There are beautiful words, thoughts, songs, and guidance from the energetic place of souls in spirit, if we listen and observe.

We Are Now in a New Spiritual Revolution

Many people, I sense, are becoming aware of their abilities or the abilities of loved ones who are expressing their gifts without fear and leading others to explore new ways to maneuver and live in the physical world.

Reiki healing and my association with gifted mediums has enabled me to be aware of life on all levels, in all energy forms, and to seek connection with others who are making every effort to bridge the gap between those who are living and those who have passed.

Will you take the ride to your personal reality and become more of the intuitive individual you were born to be? Will you seek to understand yourself and those around in a more profound, gratifying way? Will you eliminate such unnecessary sadness, anger, and fear, and replace it with more joy, acceptance, gratitude, and love?

You do not have to accept this challenge. God gave us free will over our own lives. In your present incarnation you might choose to focus on your physical existence. Not to worry, you'll likely have another incarnation to deal with the lessons! However, if you do choose to accept the challenge this time around, you must begin to entertain new ways of viewing your energetic thoughts and actions, and improve the quality of your presence in this world. If you do this simple task, you will ultimately see the world change and shift into a new and better reality, not only for yourself, but ultimately for the generations to follow.

7

∞

You Are
Not Alone

We hold these truths to be self-evident, that all men are
created equal, that they are endowed by their Creator with
certain unalienable Rights, that among these are
Life, Liberty and the pursuit of Happiness.

—Declaration of Independence
July 4, 1776

Y ou may be wondering why I began this chapter with a line from
the Declaration of Independence; after all, the Declaration is
not usually considered a spiritual document. However, these words,
written so long ago by our Founding Fathers, serve to remind us
that no one has the right to control our thoughts or actions. Just as
the Founding Fathers freed the colonies from the shackles of the
Crown, each of us must throw off our own shackles to follow our
inner values and the connection to Source that dwells in our wills
and hearts at all times.

Of course, in order to do this, we who are practicing mediums
and healers must realize our responsibility for both our physical
lives and spiritual growth. God's greatest gift was the free will to
make our own choices, but with this gift comes an awesome responsibility for what we have called forth in our lives.

As we begin to embrace our spiritual gifts and oneness with God,
we find that we have more energy, more joy, and more passion for
life. For although we are always connected to Spirit, many of us live
for years, even decades, without feeling it. When we do at last realize this connection, we feel a new sense of purpose and want to help

111

uplift others through love and our vision of the lightness of being. As human beings, our first instinct is to share this new awareness with others, especially those we hold dear. But to our dismay, we often find that those around us are not nearly as enthusiastic about our transformation as we are; they may even react negatively to it. As we change, our relationships with friends, spouses, parents—even our children—begin to change as well, and in ways that range from uncomfortable to downright painful. This is why many of us, even in the midst of our greatest connection, feel so utterly alone.

Changes in Relationships with Family and Friends as a Result of Our Spiritual Practices

We are *not* alone, of course. Each of us has scores of loving friends, relatives, angels, and guides on the other side, as well as here on the Earth plane, reaching out to us even as we are reaching for them. Patient and loving, they are there to assist us with our every need and desire. But that does not make it any easier when we can no longer relate to the best friend we have known since high school or the spouse sleeping next to us at night. When we express our new awareness, they might react with disbelief, mockery, or even disdain. Even as the Divine in us is rejoicing at this shift in consciousness, the humanness in us experiences feelings of loss, loneliness, and anger, both at ourselves for "rocking the boat" in our relationships, and at others for not agreeing to "come along for the ride."

While these reactions are normal on the human plane, they are not productive, and in order to progress in our spiritual work it is critical that we learn how to deal with changing or lost relationships. Just as important is that we build a new community that reflects our growth. Fortunately, social media, blogs, and online communities make it easier than ever to connect with like-minded people around the world.

When I began to function as a medium, my teachers repeatedly told me that a higher vibration was necessary to receive information from a spiritual dimension. As mentioned before, it took me a while to realize that attaining this higher vibration meant eliminating negativity, selfishness, fear, and an overall attachment to the physical world. This does not mean, however, that I am immune to the relationship challenges we all face.

As a person studying how to use energetic influences for my highest good and the highest good of others, I sometimes forget that I am still human. While I try to be more proactive and less reactive in my interactions with others, I occasionally find myself responding with fear to the triggers I learned as a child. I am not perfect, but a work in progress and I still find it difficult to stand by and do nothing when I am a witness to suffering.

Recently, I was once again reminded of my humanity. During a Reiki session one evening, I clearly heard the sounds of doves cooing. How odd, I thought, to hear doves at night! I asked the others in the room whether they heard it, but no one had. I knew it was a sign, but I wasn't sure what Spirit was trying to tell me. A few days later, I was still thinking about the doves when I saw a children's book called *Wings to Fly* in the reception area of my office. The cover was blue and had a penguin with tiny little wings. I had some time before leaving for my group meeting at the Academy of European Art and Culture, so I sat down to read. *Wings to Fly* was the story of a young penguin who wished to soar through the sky like other birds he had seen. He knew this wasn't possible for a bird of the land and water; still, he held the dream in his heart.

One night, he heard sounds on the lake and went to see what was happening. Santa and his sled had crashed into the middle of the lake! The penguin swam out to the sled to help. Santa warned him that it was too big a task for him, but the little penguin's courage enabled him to pull the sled to safety. The next evening, in his sleep, the penguin saw ten white doves. Gathering around him, the beautiful doves helped lift the little penguin up so he could fly.

I was struck by the parallel between life and this sweet and noble story. First, the penguin had an intention. Soon after he set the intention, a situation arose where he was able to show his best soul effort. Then, with the help of a higher power or energy, he was able to accomplish his fondest goal.

Another thing that struck me was the timing of the story, for that day I was feeling extremely sad at having been harsh with a friend. I'd made a judgment about what I perceived to be that person's involvement with certain people and unproductive situations. Like the little penguin, I felt this friend had the ability to rise above his personal challenges, but did not realize his own personal power, strengths, and unique gifts. Despite all I had learned about surrendering my will and accepting others without emotion, I had told this person to correct his thinking and his actions.

I was still distressed when I arrived at the academy, and it must have been written all over my face, because Annalisa, one of the other women in the group, noticed immediately. I told her I had spoken out of turn to a friend and was feeling bad about it. True to form, Annalisa didn't judge, but said only that perhaps I'd said what I was supposed to say.

Sometimes, when we truly wish to help another person, we allow spirit to guide us and even speak through us. We are allowing ourselves to be a clear channel, putting our agenda aside long enough for wisdom and clarity to be imparted. Sometimes when a person receives a truthful and caring statement from a friend, or even a foe, the message can be a way to help, even if it is shocking. Annalisa reminded me of this.

"Whether you spoke from your ego and intellect or from your soul thoughts, it is done," she said. Knowing she was right, I took a deep breath, let it go, and brought my presence to the meeting.

This particular group studied the interactions between a person's ego-oriented life and their soul life, much like the mystery schools of ancient Greece and Rome. The members explore the belief that the duality of our physical manifestations and the needs of our higher selves create the dysfunction and pain in our lives. Only when all aspects of our physical and energetic parts are in balance can we truly be whole, well, and deriving the best from life.

The group began with a quiet meditation. I sweetly remembered my granddaughter Samantha sitting in her booster seat, smiling serenely, holding her arms out and telling me she was flying. That had happened two days before. I also thought about the sounds of the birds that I had heard during the Reiki session, and the small blue book about the penguin who wished to fly. These things were all in my thoughts, even in this quiet time of meditation.

Suddenly, I heard birds cooing again. This time the others heard it too. One woman spoke of the connection between the sound of the birds and the Holy Spirit, the dove of peace. I smiled at the realization of what Spirit had been trying to tell me. I had indeed acted with my friend in the highest interest of all and was being blessed and forgiven, if in fact any forgiveness was needed. A higher power was forgiving me for my human frailties. The dark feelings receded from my soul, and the rest of the meeting was filled with the poetry, music, and discourse shared by like-minded people trying to balance their physical thoughts, ideas, and feelings with higher vibrations of love and dignity.

As this story shows, there are times when it is appropriate to intervene in another's behavior to protect them or others. The key is to distinguish when we are being guided by Spirit and when we are speaking from our own ego or "humanness." This is an ongoing challenge, even for intuitives, who know taking action is for the highest good of those concerned. We may have control over some of our choices in helping others, but must learn to know when to intervene or not. At times, we may be unable to act for the highest good of those we love the most.

Most of the time, the best solution is to let a person discover what is best for themselves, in their own time. This means reserving judgment, regardless of our own personal opinion or feelings, for often we don't know all the facts and karmic connections involved. Stepping back and allowing the situation to unfold restores the individual's personal responsibility and allows them the experience needed for spiritual growth.

When you accept the fact that there is a higher plan for each and every soul, you'll find you no longer try to influence an outcome, but are comfortable providing loving, *silent* support (unless specifically asked for advice). When you come to this point, you are not only doing a wonderful service for others, you will have also turned a corner in your own development.

In addition to our family and friends, we come into contact with many other people who are operating at a lower vibrational level. This can be the guy at the deli, the person standing next to us on the bus, the colleague who does not treat us with respect, and others who are not ready to transform their lives. This is not said in judgment, for each of us has our own path to follow. However, it is important to recognize these people and prevent them from draining your energy.

Methods to Achieve Balance, Courage, and Self-Confidence in Pursuit of Our Life Goals

Life is about loving what is, which is never perfect—just in a state of conscious change. If we forget about perfection and just *be*, we will find love in our journey. Everything is perfect for self-discovery, thus perfection is the ability to accept imperfection. There is no normal or abnormal, and no one way to live, love, or develop our own personal paths. We are all dealing with wounds from this as well as previous incarnations, and as such are wounded citizens of the Cosmos.

When we are born into this life, we unknowingly carry within our soul energy past-life memories of people, places, and events that resulted in less than desirable, if not devastating, outcomes. The important thing to remember is that in this *life* we can make new choices that will release these traumas to create better health and relationships and find a connection to universal energy. In order to do this, we must work towards relinquishing blame, judgment, fear, and ideas of our limitations. It is only when we create within ourselves a sense of personal power, courage, self-love, and bravery that we can embrace both the gift of life and the challenges that the universe offers us.

Along the way, we will all have experiences we perceive as negative: divorce, loss of love or friendship, painful confrontations or betrayal in professional or family situations, and illness. The important thing to understand is that while any of these events may seem difficult in the present moment, once you understand that even our most challenging experiences are opportunities for spiritual expansion, you will experience an enormous shift in awareness.

As you are going through this process, there are methods that can help you achieve a strong body, peaceful mind, and joyful heart. They can also guide and inform you as you begin to know yourself, this world, and the world beyond with clarity, hope, faith, and trust. Below are some of the tools I have found especially helpful in my own spiritual growth, as well as in my practice as a Medium and Reiki Master Teacher.

The following techniques are best done each morning and evening. They can also be done throughout the day whenever you're feeling unsettled, anxious, or are faced with a challenging situation. They might seem difficult at first, but don't be discouraged. Soon you will be able to drop into this state easily and whenever necessary. Remember that consistency in any behavior brings about whatever we wish to manifest and create for our happiness and highest good.

Rope of Life

Begin in a comfortable seated position with your spine straight. Now envision thick ropes coming from the chakras of the feet and going into the crust and mantle of the Earth below. Imagine that the heavy anchor of a ship reaches the core of the earth and grounds you to the life force of the planet.

Begin breathing slowly and deeply and imagine that you are bringing up, through the rope, the life-giving minerals and water that sustain the planet and all its life forms. Feel this essence move up the chakra system: from the root chakra to the sacral chakra, then up to the solar plexus chakra, heart chakra, throat chakra, third eye chakra, and finally, the crown chakra that resides on the top of your head.

Now imagine that you are bringing the energy of the universe in through your crown chakra. I always visualize this energy in the form of a white light. Send this white light spiraling down to join with the Earth's energy. You are now creating a state of healing, peace, and calmness that will allow the body to rest and the energies within you to awaken your inner guidance system. With regular practice, you will begin to become aware of what is necessary for your every day experiences. It will also improve your physical health, allowing you to deal with stress, pain, and interactions with others while maintaining your personal power and without robbing you of valuable energy. You will be able to resist the negativity and the controlling thoughts or actions of others who are not operating in a heightened state of connection and alignment to Spirit.

Zip It Up

It is an absolute truth that all people are connected to God and to each other. This is easy to forget as we go about our daily lives, but the fact is that these invisible energetic cords that bind us together are always affecting us, either positively or negatively. Until we understand this, we will be subject to pain, disease, and dysfunction in our relationships. Therefore, I suggest this visualization for added fortification of your body and soul energy: think of pulling a zipper up from the root chakra all the way up to your chin. This will shelter you from toxins in the environment, as well as from people vibrating at a lower frequency.

Nowhere are these exercises more important than in heavily trafficked public places. Malls, universities, and health facilities, to name a few, contain a lot of energies, many of which are troubled, angry, emotionally challenged (i.e., with mood disorders), or simply insecure and unhappy. When in places like these, I strongly recommend that in addition to doing all of the above, you visualize yourself in a suit of protective armor that covers the crown of your head, sinus area, chest, and solar plexus.

Cleansing Body and Soul

After the day's experiences, you may wish to release any thoughts that were disruptive to your natural state of joy and happiness. Visualization is a tool used by hypnotherapists, neuropsychologists, and energy healers and is very effective in entraining the brain to release limiting thoughts and behavior, thereby allowing more practical and useful behavior to become automatically part of the brain patterns. Being able to recognize the disruptive pattern and then being able to restructure your feelings to a state of peace; feeling neutral and unruffled from any event, will eventually become automatic and easy.

One visualization technique you might begin with is to envision yourself standing under a beautiful waterfall. Imagine the cool, clear, water running over your body from the head down. Visualize the water running inside your body as well, washing away and releasing any negative attachments that have come into your energy field. Most importantly, allow yourself to feel the joy of the connection to both the Great Spirit above and the Earth below.

The shower is a great place to cleanse your spirit as well as your body. As you stand under the water, call down the energy to strengthen the internal core and chakra system. Visualize the water filtering out any attachments from the night before, including those you may have encountered while in the dream state. You will find you're able to begin the day with a vibrant smile and an expectation of wonderful new experiences and adventures. If you are showering at the end of the day, perform this exercise to wash away any negative energies or thoughts you have come into contact with in your daily experience.

Protecting while Connecting

There are many different forms of meditation that will help you connect with God, as well as your angels and spirit guides. It is a sacred time to pray, ask questions, and simply relax into the universal flow. It is also the time when we need the most protection. During meditation, our chakras are wide open, making us especially receptive to energies both of this planet and beyond. Since we only wish to tap into higher vibrational beings, loved ones, and spiritual teachers who will assist us with our questions and health situations, we must protect ourselves from other energies. Before entering a state of meditation or prayer, make sure you are in a quiet place where you will not be interrupted by family, friends, or colleagues. This includes silencing your phone. Then visualize white light enveloping and protecting you during your meditation.

Recharge through Solitude

Another way to "recharge" after coming into contact with negative energies is to spend time alone. Many people find it helpful to listen to music, read, exercise, walk in nature, or utilize water through drinking, bathing, and observation of an ocean, lake, or river. Traveling the vast deserts, mountains, valleys, and cities of this beautiful Earth is another way for us to unite with our inner source of connection to all life. It also gives us an opportunity to explore different cultures, traditions, and belief systems so that we may become more accepting of others.

If it is difficult to find time for these protection techniques during your busy day, please try harder to make that extra effort. It is extremely beneficial, while also necessary, to do these exercises during the day and before going to sleep. Your success will be in accordance with the effort you put out. When lying in bed, ask that during the night you receive guidance and healing so you will be stronger and balanced in your approach to the new day.

With regular practice, these grounding and protection exercises will bring about an improvement in your state of mind, as well as your physical body. Remember, though, that you must be consistent and, above all, trust the process, for you are building and creating a better you in alignment with All That Is, Was, and Will Be.

Helping Clients to Heal from Problems in Intimate Relationships

Over the years, many of my clients have expressed sadness about their inability to manifest and maintain loving, intimate relationships. Every soul seeks to love and be loved, but there are skills and a certain level of awareness that must be developed in order to draw the right connections to you. There is a direct correlation between your current level of ability to love and your behavior that influences the progress or lack of progress in your relationship.

The expression, "Birds of a feather flock together," or "Like finds like," have some credibility. It is important to understand that when a husband or wife, boyfriend or girlfriend, friends, or siblings blame each other for the problems they are experiencing, they are merely projecting what they feel inside and are expressing this through their behavior. They may be unable to see this action and reaction, but it is at work nonetheless. It is often easier to blame another than to change yourself; however, changing yourself is the only option if you want to get off the rollercoaster ride of toxic or unsatisfying relationships.

The first step to healing your relationships is to recognize this truth: the only person that can hurt you *is* you. We hurt ourselves when we allow others to impose their will upon us, whether physically, verbally, or sexually.

We cannot control others, but we can free ourselves of their toxic behavior by holding onto our own truths, finding our own path, and consistently making choices rooted in love rather than fear, hatred, or the desire for revenge.

Many of us find that certain situations or relationship dynamics repeatedly show up in our lives. These are lessons designed by Spirit for our growth, and once we've learned them, they will disappear from our lives as if by magic to make way for something better.

That said, some relationships are not meant to last for our entire lives. Indeed, they will last only as long as necessary for the soul to grow. When they end, we must look past the appearance of pain, recognize the lesson, and move on. Do not dwell on the appearance of "failure," for there is no such thing. There are only experiences leading ultimately to our highest good.

Techniques to Improve Communication in Relationships of Love

The Divine Source encompasses both the masculine and the feminine, hence the terms "Father God" and "Mother Earth." Men and women are the human manifestation of these male and female energies. But while it is true that we are all aspects of Source, it is also true that men and women exhibit different energy, interests, hormonal structures, needs, and obligations. In addition, each of us has male and female energies, in varying degrees. It is in utilizing both energies that we become well-functioning individuals and can recognize the unique qualities, whether male or female, of others.

According to a study from the United Kingdom University of Sheffield, there are even differences in the way men and women process the sound of the human voice. "Men's brains hear women's voices first as music, but it is not music … so the brain goes into overdrive trying to analyze what is being said … It's not the pitch, but rather the vibration and number of sound waves that cause the problem." The study also claims that, "men have to work harder deciphering what women are saying because they use the auditory part of the brain that processes music, not human voices." *

These differences often result in friction and miscommunication that can destroy even a loving connection. Only by trying to understand the true natures of the male and female personas and the strengths and weaknesses of an imbalanced energy can we learn to love and accept others as we are.

To encourage a better flow of communication between men and women, we must keep these physical differences in mind. Many of my female clients have told me that the men in their lives don't listen to them. I gently explain to these women that this may be a simple misunderstanding of the dynamics of male and female energy. I advise them that when speaking with their husbands or boyfriends, sons, fathers, or grandfathers, they should first say exactly what they mean and then allow the men time to go into another room to unwind and process what was said. I've often found that after they've had this time, they can be approached again with the same question or discussion with a lot less friction.

---

* "Why Men Don't Listen to Women." *Netscape Men's*. NeuroImage, n.d. Web. 24 Sept. 2013.<http://webcenters.netscape.compuserve.com/men/package.jsp ?name=fte/womenspeak/womenspeak>.

Timing Is Everything

Choose a time when you are both alert, this way you will be more receptive to what the other is saying. According to Marianne J. Legato, MD, "Men don't multitask as well as women and this may be related to the fact that in general women activate more areas in their brain than men do when performing identical tasks." Legato points out that initiating a discussion while your partner is watching television or surfing the Internet probably means you will not receive his full attention.

Mind Your Words

How you begin the discussion is equally as important. Improving communication with your partner means opening every discussion with a positive statement, rather than criticism. If you are facing a challenge in this regard, ask Spirit to guide "for the highest good of all concerned."

Honor Your Partner's Path

Throughout this process we must remember that while following our spiritual path we must also allow others to follow their own. It is unrealistic to expect our loved ones to share in all of our passions and activities. True love allows the other to explore their needs and to grow according to their own plan and in their own time. Those who cannot achieve this desired state of being with their loved ones need to work on their own controlling behavior, either within the confines of the relationship or by seeking help from a trained professional. Each of us must learn that we cannot hold a bird in our hands and restrict it from its normal desire to fly. Similarly, love cannot be held too tightly, but must be allowed to grow as each person strives to discover and use his or her own Divine gifts.

Know When to Let It Go

Once you have honestly done all you could to improve your behavior, control issues, and unrealistic expectations, it is time to offer the issue up to Spirit. We cannot have expectations of anyone other than ourselves, so if the relationship still lacks the qualities necessary for health and love, it may have simply run its course. Despite what your family, friends, or society may believe, there is no disgrace or failure associated with ending a relationship. On the contrary, it frees both parties to find other opportunities for love and growth. So rather than holding onto something that was not meant to last, try letting go of all blame, anger, and frustration and look forward to the new experiences coming your way. It will save you months or even years of needless suffering.

I am reminded through a message, unsolicited and given to me by international medium, Peter Close, that my father, Myron, had a message for me, and it was quite different from the belief that he had expressed when alive. My father believed divorce was unacceptable and tragic, but now in Spirit he realized divorce or broken relationships were at times a necessary event of the physical life. My dad no longer had any judgment about people needing to make that decision.

Protecting Ourselves from Negative Emotions of Damaged and Toxic People

When following your spiritual path it is critical that you learn to avoid being vulnerable from damaged or toxic people and to emote greater, loving feelings to help in their healing. These individuals operate on a low vibrational frequency, and many of them are quite comfortable doing so. Perhaps they resonated with you at some point in your life, but as you seek your own truth and enlightenment they will keep you stagnant and rooted in old beliefs that you need to shed in order to move to the next level. They can also drain you of the positive energy and joy that is your natural state and God-given right.

These people are functioning through their egos, not their souls, and are therefore at a loss to understand themselves or others. They exist in a perpetual state of fear and pain and often seek relief by draining the energy of others. To fill the void in their own lives, they try to bring others down by creating friction, drama, and discomfort. Hence the well-known phrase, "misery loves company." They have not figured out that the answer to greater happiness lies within themselves.

Those who are not plugged into the positive energies of the Divine tend to draw their satisfaction and energy from other more spiritually-developed people. Whether they realize it or not, they want what the spiritually-minded person has. However, since they don't know how to get it, they achieve their "good feelings" through manipulative interactions. These satisfying feelings last for a very short time, and then these people get another "fix" by sucking energy from someone else. That's why one often feels tired and anxious when around controlling or victimizing personalities.

I read an article in *O, The Oprah Magazine*, identifying five types of "energy vampires." We all come across these people in our daily lives, but although all five types cause damage, not all are easily recognizable. One example was a newly hired female executive. The woman seemed nice enough, until one day she launched a horrific verbal attack on the office assistant, who'd had a recent miscarriage. The executive criticized and yelled at her for having missed time at work, and even for having the "audacity" to become pregnant in the first place. The assistant burst into tears and everyone else looked on in shock, for they had never seen this side of the executive before.

There is never a reason to harm another person by losing control. A person who shows such a lack of sensitivity needs to do it only once for his or her true character to be exposed. Thankfully, it was not long after this incident that the higher-ups in the company observed other lapses in this executive's work ethic and fired her.

There are many people who function in an underhand way because of their insecurities. The key is to recognize and detach whenever possible from these types of situations and people. We must only focus on the positive, as that will help the negative aspect to fall away from us.

Emotions, whether positive ones like excitement and enthusiasm, or uncomfortable ones like sadness, fear, and anger, are contagious. This goes back to the point I made earlier about everyone being energetically connected. These connections are like powerful cords that keep us "tuned in" to each other's emotions. There are certain people who, consciously or not, want to make you feel as low as they do. These emotional bullies get their power by inflicting their moods, negativity, and anger on others, making them dangerous to the well-being of everyone around them.

Recognizing people with personality or mood disorders involving extreme narcissism or a diagnosis of bipolar disease or borderline personality is not always easy to do, as people with these conditions often hide them well. Yet they still manage to create tremendous problems in the home and at work.

In addition to energy vampires, we also must beware of drama queens and chronic complainers. Who among us has not had a friend, relative, or coworker who consistently drained us of our life energy? After unleashing a storm of toxic emotions, these people often walk away happy and unaffected and leave us, the traumatized victim, in their wake. Thankfully, there are exercises we can all use to cut the cords and protect our hearts.

The More the Merrier

The most effective strategy is to avoid one-on-one interaction with people who exhibit negative behavior. If you have a friend who tends to infect you with her negative moods, invite others to make it a group outing. If this doesn't work, suggest an activity such as seeing a movie, shopping, or visiting a museum. This will limit the time for conversation and her opportunity to unload her unhappiness or negativity onto you.

Walk a Tightrope

Sometimes we cannot avoid negative people, particularly in work situations. However, there are other tools to keep you from internalizing another's toxic energy. When your negative colleague is careening out of control, it is often helpful to say, "Why don't we change the subject?" If it's your boss spewing this verbal garbage, try focusing on a calming thought, such as "I am not going to let this get to me," or whatever you find works for you. Another thing you can do is pay careful attention to your own physical responses. If you feel anxious or heaviness on the heart or in the head, this is a sure sign that you're in the presence of uncontrolled anger, rage, jealousy, envy, or other lower vibrational emotions.

The next time you find yourself in a situation like this, move several steps away from the person to determine if it is indeed the energy and emotion emitted from this person or something else happening around you creating this discomfort. If you feel better immediately, then you know it is the energy of that person. If you continue to feel unsettled in your body, then it is the energy in the place or location.

Whatever the cause, it is time to take preventative action to ensure your own personal comfort. Take a few deep breaths, breathing deeply into the solar plexus. This will help ground you into your own solid state. You may also use any of the protection and grounding exercises I discussed earlier to help you ward off a psychic or verbal attack from this person. If you continue to feel uncomfortable, try to remove yourself from the location.

DO NOT ENGAGE

It is very important not to engage in the other person's negative behavior. Do not fight, yell, or otherwise allow yourself to be pulled into an argument. Remain neutral, even if it means excusing yourself. If you cannot physically leave the situation, *Positive Energy* author Dr. Judith Orloff recommends that you imagine there is a shield or wall around you. You will still hear what the other person is saying, but the emotions behind their words won't get under your skin.

BALANCE IT OUT

After you've spent time with people who may be displaying the behavior due to a mood disorder, anxieties, or other negative emotions, make it a point to spend time with nurturing, positive people that can help return you to a state of balance.

FLIP IT ON 'EM

Here are a few other things you can do to protect yourself. When a person's words begin to overwhelm you, suggest in a neutral tone that you talk about something else. It is important to be kind and honest, but never accusatory, as this will only engage them further. When someone asks you a question that you feel is out of line, intrudes upon your personal space, or that you simply do not want to answer, just look them in the eye and ask, "Why do you want to know?"

No matter how adept we become at protecting ourselves from the negative energy of others, chances are there will still be times when we are upset by the words or actions of others. This often depends on the significance this person has in our lives. Regardless of who it is, you need to trust your intuition. If you feel that they are trying to push your buttons, disturb your peace, or steal your joy, disengage immediately. Simply refuse to be brought into their energy.

The key is to realize that each person perceives the world according to his or her experiences, from this life *and* past incarnations. Therefore, we cannot hope to understand every aspect of another's behavior. Remember that we are all spiritual beings having a human experience; everyone is trying—on various levels—to find their own way. All you can do is stay in a positive state of allowing and accepting love. The goal is acceptance, of everything and everyone, without judgment, anxiety, fear, pain, anger, hate, or any negative feeling. Peace and bliss are then not only possible, but *probable!*

8

∞

Now and Forever: Guidance from the Other Side

The past is but the beginning of a beginning,
and all that is and has been is but the twilight of the dawn.

—H. G. Wells, *The Discovery of the Future* (1901)

Everyone can recall having at least one flash of intuition. It may have been a strong feeling, or as subtle as a breeze on a hot summer day, but it was there. It may have assisted you in making a good decision or prevented you from making a poor one. Perhaps you knew—just *knew*—that something was going to happen, only to get confirmation an hour, a day, or a week later that it had indeed occurred. Most people write it off as a "coincidence" or perhaps "good luck," but that could not be further from the truth. These feelings are the whispers from Spirit, the support of our family and friends on the Other Side.

We also have spirit guides who are aware of the plan, not only for our present incarnation, but the dharmic plan for our souls. "Dharma" is an ancient word rooted in Sanskrit, and is a multifaceted concept central to both Hinduism and Buddhism. It embodies "laws" of spiritual living while in the physical world, but it also includes the eternal path of the soul over many earthly incarnations. But how do we know what our dharmic path is? After all, it's hard enough to know what our path is for *one* lifetime!

As I mentioned earlier, each of us is presented with a series of life experiences and lessons learned from them are for the benefit of our own souls. In fact, *we* chose these experiences because of the lessons we would learn before we were born onto this earthly plane—difficult to believe when we are faced with highly unpleasant circumstances. But choose them we did, and the way we deal with these experiences and lessons we gain from them determines how close we get to accomplishing our goals for this incarnation, as well as our overall dharmic path.

Receiving Help from Our Spiritual Guides

That's where our guides come in. Part of their mission is to support us as we go through the lessons. In this way, they help us uncover the plan, step by step, so that we can develop our souls while serving humanity.

Whatever else you take away from this book, know this: the ability to quiet the mind and transcend your human ego is essential to hearing from your guides and thus learning certain spiritual truths. Over the years, my guides have consistently led me to new levels of healing abilities and mediumship. Most of these "meetings" have taken place during meditation, when I am able to quiet my human personality and travel to other spiritual realms. I always return with another piece of knowledge, another piece of the puzzle that allows me to move forward in service to others. One might think that after practicing meditation for so many years that I might find it commonplace. In reality, nothing could be further from the truth. Each new experience leaves me in complete and utter awe at the power of Source and the ever-expanding beauty of the Universe.

My son, Gregg, arranged a vacation for our entire family to meet in Kennebunk, Maine, where he and my daughter, Stacey, had rented a house. The trip was planned around the wedding of one of Gregg's college friends.

Over the past few years, I had seen Gregg help many of his friends find work and refine their relationships. All of them seemed intent on moving into the future together and collaborating on plans to enjoy and advance their families, careers, and communities. In fact, both my children had several friends who were developing into conscientious and conscious members of the community and finding their own spiritual realities for co-creating good lives. I had known most of them since they were children and was grateful for the opportunity to observe their growth, particularly since it seemed indicative of the greater evolution of humanity.

This particular trip had been planned for many months. My daughter and her family—her husband, Jeremy, the four girls, and their au pair, Gaby—would be driving six hours from their home in New Jersey. They had found a wonderful house that was beautiful and large enough to sleep twelve people. There was only one flaw: no air-conditioning. The day before we were scheduled to fly to Maine, Gregg called to tell me that it had been unusually hot there—an extreme heat wave. He felt that David and I would be more comfortable staying in a nearby inn. I readily agreed, for I had found that since becoming an energy healer, I had become increasingly affected by shifts in my physical environment, including extreme weather on both ends of the spectrum.

David and I boarded the plane, and I settled into an aisle seat. The woman next to me was also heading to Maine for a family outing. She would be meeting her newborn granddaughter for the first time. When she mentioned that she was a nurse, I said that I was an energy healer and had worked as a hospice volunteer for years. She was interested to hear how Reiki was used in conjunction with traditional medicine, as well as how it can help bring people comfort as they prepare to leave the earthly plane.

"My name is Cookie," she said, offering me a hand and a friendly grin.

I smiled back. "I have four little granddaughters and I always call them 'Cookie girls.'" This small but pleasant synchronicity reminded me how often I met people who shared my passion for helping others, albeit using different methods.

When our flight landed, Gregg was waiting to bring David and me to the inn. It was a lovely place, nestled among giant trees. Nearby, a small inlet filled and emptied each day according to the ebb and flow of the ocean. It was truly a place of peace and beauty, with the large trees reaching forever upward and rolling hills that extended well beyond my vision. A small pool was right outside the doorway, and since we had some time before Gregg returned to take us to the house, I put on my bathing suit and bounced joyfully down the steps to the pool area. It was not crowded; only three women were seated at the far end. I closed my eyes and relaxed, feeling the warm sun on my body, delighted to be in such a beautiful, serene setting.

When I opened my eyes, I saw light—or, more accurately, an energetic life force—emanating from the giant tree directly in front of me. The light danced from the base of the tree through all the branches and leaves. Amazing!

I suddenly recalled reading James Redfield's *The Celestine Prophecy* several years before. The energy from the tree was exactly as that book had described: the illuminating life force of all living things. When I was reading it, I had assumed that the description was simply part of the author's poetic, beautiful way of creating an awareness of light. Now, years later, after extensive years of training and practice as an energy healer, I felt and sensed the energy flow within myself and observed the projections of energy through the thoughts and actions of others.

In a meditative state, I had often observed the colors shift and intensify as they were reflected within the chakra channels of a person's body, as well as the aura surrounding the body. However, this was the first time that I visually observed the energy of a tree! It seemed inconceivable, but I could not deny what I was seeing: movement of energy, from the base of the roots up the entire length and beyond the reach of its branches. I could not take my eyes off the miraculous vision.

I was still in awe when the sight faded a few minutes later. The three women were still at the other end of the pool, and I found myself walking over to them, introducing myself, and telling them what I had just seen. I was not thinking about whether they would have an awareness or understanding of such matters; I just wanted to share my experience. After describing the movement of the energy force through the roots, branches, and leaves of the tree, I asked if any of them had read *The Celestine Prophecy*. One of the women, a tall, beautiful, blonde, said, "Yes I have." She told me she was a nurse. I smiled to myself remembering the nurse named Cookie I had just met on the plane ride and thought how interesting it is when these coincidences occur. And here I met a mother and her two grown daughters and I was soon to meet up with my two grown children.

My son and daughter each had their own children, a total of four girls and one boy ranging in age from seven months to five years. Yet, I often thought of events from Stacey and Gregg's childhood, which still seemed to exist in the here and now. As a medium, it is a wonderful reminder that the past, present, and even the future, are always accessible.

Seeing and Meeting Master Spirit Guides to Relay Their Messages

After spending the afternoon with the family in the very hot rental house, I was delighted to return to my hotel room and sleep with air-conditioning. The next morning at breakfast, David and I were waited on by a friendly young woman named Jill. We happened to be the only people in the restaurant, and after the meal Jill stayed by the table to chat with us.

She mentioned that she had recently had her gallbladder removed but still had some ongoing digestive issues. I suggested to Jill that energy work could assist in her recovery and improve her general health. She excitedly told me that Carol, another waitress I had met earlier, was a Polarity Healer.

Smiling, I explained to Jill that this was synchronicity at its best. We had met on a morning when she just "happened" to have time to chat; she told me about her medical problems, I suggested energy healing, and—lo and behold!—she already knew an energy healer. Perhaps she would have gone to Carol eventually, perhaps not. But through our conversation, Spirit was giving her a nudge in that direction. I suggested that she work with Carol, both so she could feel better and so she could gain understanding of her own energy patterns.

Jill ran back to the kitchen, and returned a moment later with Carol who said to me, "I was aware when I saw you that you were someone I was meant to meet and share some time with," then added matter-of-factly, "I see people's guides."

"You see people's guides?" I was in awe. I had on occasion seen clients' guides or relatives when I did the readings prior to their healing session. However, it was not the focus of my healing practice and not a regular occurrence. While we all have spiritual gifts, some stronger than others, it is always exciting to learn about the specialized abilities of others.

"Who is you master guide?" I asked Carol.

"David," she replied as if she were talking about her best friend, "a soul from a past life."

I nodded and said, "I believe we have three master guides at the time of our birth, and over the course of our life, specialized guides come in to assist us with our changing needs and experiences."

"Do you know your guide?" Carol asked.

"I've had a sense of my guides from time to time." I said cryptically, for although I did indeed have a notion of who my guides were, I hesitated to reveal the identity, as I thought some might see it as preposterous, pretentious, or even arrogant.

Carol paused for a beat and then blurted out, "Your guide is Jesus, and in your new book you should state this."

For a moment, I sat there, completely shocked by what she had said. Then I found myself holding back tears, for she had validated what I had believed for some time. What an awesome reminder, both of my soul's growth and the responsibility for my own personal development! Moreover, I also felt she was validating my soul's purpose: helping others rise above the limitations of their physical lives to realize they are Divine, eternal beings of the Universe.

In truth, I should not have been surprised to hear an ancient healer was looking over me. I believe that Jesus and other Divine souls act as the guides for many who are exploring healing, energy dynamics, and manifesting. Years before, a Native American shaman had told me that my guide was a healer and ancient father figure, who had been with me for many lifetimes.

Carol went on to say she was glad I was on the planet at this time because many people needed me. I was encouraged by her enthusiasm and her honesty. As she hugged me, I offered to send her a copy of my first book, *Life Is No Coincidence: The Life and Afterlife Connection*. And I told her that I was indeed working on my second book, *The Living Spirit: Answers for Healing and Infinite Love*.

Responding to Those Who Ask Our Help to Heal

We returned home on Labor Day, and I had barely walked in the door when my phone started ringing. It was Gertrude, an old friend and fellow religious, spiritual, and scientific explorer. We have helped each other define our lives in relation to others and to the greater Universal life. Now, however, Gertrude was telling me that she had fallen and needed a treatment.

"What kind of treatment?" I asked, as she had been receiving craniosacral sessions regularly for the past twelve years.

Gertrude said, "I need what you do, Reiki, and would you please do a reading for me too?"

"Sure, I can do that. I'll be right over." I had learned over the years that I must respond immediately and without hesitation, whenever and wherever I am asked. Upon returning home, I reflected on Gertrude's choice of words, "I need you." Carol, the Polarity healer from Maine, had said that people would need me. I found it extremely curious that immediately upon returning home I had heard those same words from my longtime friend.

The very next morning I received another important call, this time from a young woman named Evelyn. I had also known her for a long time, at least eight years. We met at Kinkos, where she was working at the time. She had helped me with the printing for my advertisements and office displays. We had spent hours together creating and producing the materials, and I found her to be a joyful, positive person.

A few years after we met, she had called to tell me her father had passed away. She wanted to come in for a reading and a healing session. As a result of that reading and lovely messages from her father in Spirit, she decided to return to school. Eventually, she also left Kinko's and got a job at a hospital.

I was surprised to hear from Evelyn, for I had not spoken to her in years. I was even more surprised when she said, "I need you. You told me years ago that I would have a daughter. Since then there have been many wonderful changes in my life. I have married a man who was a longtime friend of mine, and a few days ago, I had my daughter, Natalie."

She then told me that Natalie had been born with a rare heart problem. We spoke for a long time, and I asked if she would like me to send distance healing for her husband, herself, and the baby. I hoped the three of them would share a bond of love and realize that all would happen according to the plan for their lives and in furtherance of their souls' expansion.

I was careful to sound positive when speaking to Evelyn, but as soon as we got off the phone, I burst into tears. I cried for this newborn soul struggling for a physical life with the mother who wanted her so badly. Knowing that the outcome was already written in the plan of their lives, I could only send them healing energy and trust that it would do what it was supposed to. I had asked Evelyn to call me and let me know how everything turned out, but I did not hear from her again. This is another lesson for everyone, particularly healers: people come into our lives seeking help, and we can only channel the energy to them and trust that whatever happens is for their Highest Good. Sometimes, we may not even know the outcome here in the physical world.

Several weeks before receiving Evelyn's phone call, I had been doing a reading for one of the members of my unfoldment group when I suddenly sensed Jesus next to me. He was crying, and I found myself choking back tears as well. "I have cried for many ills done by unknowing souls," Jesus said, "just as you and your group members also cry for the injustice and insensitivity of many."

Several other members of the group, including Joyce, who I was reading at that time, sensed his presence. His words to me brought a feeling to my heart that to this day is hard to describe. It was incredible to think that he would visit a simple Reiki teacher and her group, reminding everyone present of the loving messages he had delivered during his earthly life so very long ago. It was as if Jesus wanted us to know that he and other emissaries of the unseen world work by our side for the continued advancement of humanity. They impress upon all of us that self-love and love for others will always be the goal for a soul experiencing a physical and energetic life. To strive for personal excellence without hypocrisy in thought, word, and action, was the message from Jesus two thousand years ago. As the world and its citizens continue to move forward, many will finally hear and truly follow Jesus's teaching to create a sense of great peace and unity for all, emanating from the Oneness of our soul being.

A few days later, on the way home from my office, I passed a church. In the window was a sign that read, "Jesus is the only insurance policy for life." To me, this suggested that one who follows the values of their inner being will realize their Divine nature and personal connection to Source, regardless of religious affiliation.

By listening to your heart and the lessons of your soul, you will indeed be aligned with the wisest communication and guidance system of all worlds. In following this wisdom, you will sustain your sense of balance, courage, integrity, and honesty, no matter what outside influences reach you.

Sensing Our Interactions in Past Lives

One year later, my family and I found ourselves planning another trip to Maine. Gregg and his wife Lea would be flying in from California, despite having had their second child, Greyson, just three months before. I wasn't surprised that they were willing to deal with the inconvenience of travelling with two babies; it is important to Gregg that his family remains close, even though we live on opposite coasts. He takes this commitment very seriously.

I now had six beautiful grandchildren, and those who were old enough to speak called me Grand-mama. It was the name I had chosen years ago when asked by my daughter how I wanted to be addressed by her kids. I didn't know why I chose the name. It had just popped into my mind after months of thought on the subject.

A few months after my first granddaughter was born, a student of mine bought me a book entitled *Anna, Woman of Miracles*. Written by Carol Haenni and Vivian Van Vick, her story of Anne, mother of the Blessed Mother Mary and grandmother of Jesus, is based on a recounting of the story of St. Anne (or Anna), the mother of Virgin Mary in early Christian apocryphal writings.

Anne—or Anna, as she is referred to throughout the book—may not be as well known as other biblical characters, but she certainly led a remarkable life. She had three husbands, three daughters all named Mary, and profound healing abilities. She also had a lifelong relationship with a Roman legate known as Julian. Although he was Roman, Julian stayed close to Anne, as his greatest wish was to protect her.

The Romans who ruled Palestine had heard a prophecy that a Jewish child would be born, a Messiah that would lead the Jews to freedom. Facing a revolution, it was decided by the powers that be to dispose of the firstborn son of each Jewish family so the prophecy could not be fulfilled. Mary had already given birth to Jesus, and Anne, desperate to save her grandson, turned to Julian for help. Julian smuggled Jesus past the guards, risking his own life to take the infant out of the city. Anne would not see her friend Julian for many years, although their connection was sacred and Divine. As the story ends, an older and wearier Roman soldier appeared in the garden looking for Anne. Jesus, now seventeen years old, received Julian into the garden and told him his "Grand-mama" would soon be home.

When I read this story, it was as if I was remembering a place long ago. Suddenly, I understood Anne's feelings of needing to be a healer, fulfilling her destiny, and honoring God's plan. The Divine whispers from Spirit always guided her to live a productive life in the service of family and humanity.

As an ancient spiritual seeker and healer, Anne was interested in personal communication with Source. She also believed in an afterlife and angelic messages. It is still true today that spiritual seekers work from their own heart essence, and not necessarily from religious scripture or structure. Whether I observed life in that time long ago, or shared stories with other souls in Spirit about those ancient people by reading *Anna, Woman of Miracles,* I was able to make great sense out of many of the demands and challenges of my personal life in this time and place.

One day, as I sat on the lovely beach in Maine with my grandchildren, I was thrilled to hear eighteen-month-old Sullivan look at me and say, "Ma Ma Ma." It was his first attempt at my nickname. Stacey's older daughters, Alea and Samantha, stood at the water's edge, while her twins, Chelsea and Talia, played in the sand with their shovels and pails.

Suddenly I noticed two women standing several feet away and to my left. With them were two teenage girls that appeared to be their daughters. The women looked so very much alike, and I called out to them, asking if they were twins.

They said that they were. However, it was immediately apparent—even from a distance—that one seemed energetically much older than the other. I walked closer to them to continue talking and noticed that the woman who appeared older had a scar on her chest. She soon disclosed to me that she had had several surgeries and radiation therapy for cancer. I asked if she had had energy healing sessions to assist in her healing regime, and she responded that she was a nurse and was very grateful to have those energy healing treatments to aid in her recovery.

I realized as I observed the twin sisters that while they were identical physically, their life choices and probably their energetic or soul influences were very different. As a result of the needs and development of their souls, their physical lives, health, relationship experiences, and their spiritual awareness, their souls' life plans were distinctively different.

Each human being builds through unity and purpose of experiences, an indivisible "ONENESS" of the finest aspects of divine blessings, which are love, humility, forgiveness, and the generosity of merging ourselves with all that is. The purpose must be to prepare and refine our souls through our choices made in our physical lives for an eternal soul life worthy of divine introspection.

As I fell asleep that night in Maine, in a place still free of the ravages of overpopulated areas where technology, mass production, and excessive pollution have endangered our precious environments, I envisioned the open majestic freshness of forest, water, and pure and happy children and families nestled amidst the beauty of this majestic natural state. I had a dream, or perhaps a visitation, from one of my loving guides in Spirit, and I heard:

Remember a place, high above my home—a land of light, which reflects the pure bright colors of the rainbow.

Remember teachers of divine beauty, love, and wisdom and hear their thoughts which sound like music to prepare you into your physical life with the finest preparation to succeed in all you do.

Remember the peace and joy, laughter and smiles, the encouragement and love in the glances from their bright inquisitive eyes.

Remember when you walk on the plains, fields, meadows, and roadways of your earth life who walks beside you and who holds your hand, and always feel loved, protected, and safe—for you are.

Remember as you watched from on high and observed yourself living the challenges of your life, you may not always have felt that you could handle the challenges, but be assured you have created and chosen your life experiences and can indeed be the master of any situation.

Remember that before beginning this life you chose your parents and grandparents, sisters and brothers, and your friends, and they will mirror both the best and worst in your own being.

Then you may choose to love them without judgment or blame.

Remember each day is perfect and necessary for you to see, feel, and embrace the energy of the places and people who share the same space.

Remember as your heart beats and your feet tap and you dance to music only you might hear from your guide or angel in an eternal place of true love, that you are never alone.

Remember to stand firmly in these safe feelings delivered to you now in life and also long before your earthly existence, and feel all those souls who walk and stand in your presence and who honor your divine soul being.

Remember you have asked to help others and yourself feel the passion and energy of joy while on the earth plane and later to carry these intelligent refined emotions when you lift up and return to the energy you originated from.

Remember words of courage from heroes who fought and died to honor all men as soul equals. Even though physical attributes and differences in ability are visible while in a physical life, still remember each person is unique and divine, neither good nor bad. Do not judge. Do not expect to find perfection in a physical life, as it is not possible.

Remember you and remember me as one together in unity and love for all time in life, and yes, in death.

As I awoke from my dream, I remembered to be grateful for my life and was happy to know that so many others are finally awakened to this awareness of their physical and spiritual lives. May we all rest in the peace of this lovely thought and finally breathe in the power of The Living Spirit available to all of us for creating a world that those above guide us to discover.

And so it is!

Epilogue

Sometimes one cannot see the long-term predictions mediums and psychics offer. The following story of Jessica's future successes, which Michael from Spirit foretold, occurred years after his death.

Shortly after Michael died from a motorcycle accident at the age of nineteen, Jessica, who was working in a beauty salon at that time, realized she wanted to use each day of her life to make a difference and to be of service towards others. Rather than retreating into her grief and negative thoughts about her future, Jessica made a courageous decision to leave New York for Texas to attend nursing school. Perhaps her Reiki sessions had helped her see her own potential as a sensitive healer and one who could, with effort, bring help to those who needed it. Two years later, having completed her nursing studies with honors, she returned to New York. Even though jobs were difficult to find, Jessica was immediately placed in a hospital in Queens, New York, in the pediatric nursing unit.

I remember Jessica saying that it would be great if I could come and give Reiki to the babies. Of course, she was not in a position to make that happen, nor was I, though I would have loved nothing more than to see well-trained and dedicated Reiki practitioners in any setting where people were experiencing life-threatening events.

While working at the hospital, there was a young Indian pediatrician who Jessica saw each morning as she finished her shift and he arrived for his. A year later, they officially met at a barbeque, and despite their opposite schedules and different cultural backgrounds, began dating. Seven years later, my husband and I received an invitation to their wedding in Cancún.

The messages I had received from Jessica's first boyfriend, Michael, shortly after his passing had strongly suggested Jessica would be happy and share a different kind of love. It was therefore

142

with great reverence and joy that I attended her and Harry's wedding. As we stood on that pier in Mexico, surrounded by the deep blue ocean, I could feel the warm breeze and knew Michael and other loved ones in Spirit watched over this glorious and loving union. It was truly, for me, a Reiki miracle, promised at the time of Michael's death and assisted by Spirit now.

In my mind and heart, I was grateful to share this moment of love. Yet as I departed Mexico, I realized that Spirit was not finished.

Jessica's sister Lauren is an attorney, and upon meeting the best man, Jessica realized Lauren knew him from law school. Harry's best man, Michael, told Lauren that he had met Harry in the second grade and had remained close ever since. These people were close and now welcomed each other, felt reunited and reminded of their deep connections to each other. It reminded me that members of our soul group have not only been with us in this lifetime, but other previous incarnations.

In the van that took me to the airport for my return flight, I mentioned to a man seated behind me that I was leaving after attending a wedding at the Excellence Hotel. The young man, an attorney from Manhattan named Matt, told me that he had also attended a friend's wedding the previous night. I explained that I was a Reiki energy healer and that the bride was my client Karen's daughter. I explained that she had lost her first boyfriend, Michael, years before, and I had done a reading to help her and his family deal with the untimely death. The messages I had received from the reading revealed that Michael showed clearly his love for the people he had to leave and that he would go forward into a new spiritual life. He communicated to me that he would always be near by with love.

As I recounted the story of the wedding, Matt told me his friend who had been married the night before was also a young man named Michael. We both saw our meeting as Spirit's way of bolstering and confirming what we already knew to be true: we are Divine, loving souls meeting those along the road of life who inspire and aid us to live and love life and its mysteries in a more comprehensive and deeper way.

In the end, there is only a new beginning and greater love.

Suggested Reading List

Adler, Andrea. *Pushing Upward*. Carlsbad, CA: Hay House Inc., 2012.

Alexander, Eben, M.D. *Proof of Heaven*. New York: Simon and Schuster, 2012.

Allison, Susan, Dr. *Empowered Healer*. Bloomington, IN: Balboa Press, 2011.

Beck, Laurie. *I Am Living To Tell*. Create Space Independent Publishing, 2012.

Bedrick, David, Esq. *Talking Back to Dr. Phil*. Santa Fe, New Mexico: Belly Song Press, 2013.

Bertoldi, Concetta. *Inside the Other Side*. New York: Harper Collins Publications, 2012.

Blackman, Sherry. *Call to Witness*. Tiburon, CA: World Press, 2013.

Brannon, Steve Rev. Dr. *The Two Agreements*. Create Space Independent Publishing, 2011.

Brown, Robert. *We Are Eternal*. New York: Warner Books Inc., 2003.

Cannon, Charles, Master. *Forgiving the Unforgiveable*. New York: SelectBooks Inc., 2012.

Cappannelli, George and Sedena. *Do Not Go Quietly*. Agape Media International LLC, 2013.

Celenza, Frank T. *The Manuel*. Pittsburg, PA: Dorrance Publishing Co. Inc., 2011.

Chase, Michael J. *Am I being kind?* Carlsbad, CA: Hay House Inc., 2011.

Cohen, Andrew. *Evolutionary Enlightenment*. New York: SelectBooks, Inc., 2011.

Coppes, Christophor. *The Essence of Religions*. New York: SelectBooks, Inc., 2013.

Dalian, Eliza Mada. *In Search of the Miraculous*. Vancouver, B.C., CA: Expanding Universe Publishing, 2012.

Dosick, Wayne, Rabbi. *The Real Name of God*. Rochester VT: Inner Traditions, 2012.

D'Rianna, Adara. "Loving Yourself Free of Charge." Rainbow
  Creators LLC., 2010
Duane, Mal. *Alpha Chick*. Framingham, MA: Alpha Chick Press,
  2012.
Edlund, Matthew, M.D. *Healthy Without Health Insurance*. USA:
  Circadian Press, 2012.
Fairfield, Peter. *Deep Happy*. MA., Newburyport, MA: Weiser Books,
  2012.
Friedel, E.Z., M.D. *Marilyn's Red Diary*. New York:,Beach Hut
  Publications, 2013.
Gewirtz, Matthew, Rabbi. *The Gift of Grief*. Berkley, CA: Celestial
  Arts, 2008.
Grant, Laurie Uri. *Transform Your Life Now*. Parker, CO: Outskirts
  Press, 2011.
Grayson, Henry, Dr. *Use Your Body to Heal Your Mind*. USA, Balboa
  Press, 2012.
Griffith- Bennett, Cindy. *Soul Soothers*. Scotland, UK: Findhorn
  Press, 2013.
Grohman, Elaine. *The Angels and Me*. Columbus, OH: Seraph
  Books, LLC, 2009.
  -*Spirit Awakening*. Farmington Hills, MI: In Light LLC, 2011.
Hamilton, David. *How Your Mind Can Heal Your Body*. UK: Hay
  House, 2008.
Harra, Carmen, Dr. *The Eleven Eternal Principles*. Berkley CA:
  Crossing Press, 2011.
  -*Everyday Karma*. New York: Ballantine Books, 2002.
  -*Wholeliness*. Carlsbad, CA: Hay House Inc., 2011.
Houston, Jean, Dr. *The Wizard of Us*. New York: Atria Books, 2012.
Hunter, Allan, Dr. *Gratitude and Beyond*. Scotland, UK: Findhorn
  Press, 2013.
Kagan, Annie, D.C. *The Afterlife of Billy Fingers*. Charlottesville, VA:
  Hampton Roads Publishing, 2013.
Karlin, Marlise. *The Power of Peace In You*. London, UK: Watkins
  Publishing, 2012.
Kelly, Mira. *Healing Through Past-Life Regression and Beyond*.
  Carlsbad, CA: Hay House Inc., 2012.

Keyes, Raven. *The Healing Power of Reiki.* Woodbury, MN: Llewellyn Publications, 2012.

Lapin, Jackie. *Practical Conscious Creation.* Scotland, UK: Findhorn Press, 2011.

Massey, Harry and Hamilton, David. *Choice Point.* UK: Hay House Inc., 2011.

McCarthy, Peter M. *Adrenaline Nation.* Petaluma, CA: Smart Publications, 2012.

McIntosh, Steve, Esq. *Evolution's Purpose.* New York: SelectBooks, 2012.

Merriwether, Craig. *Depression 180.* Hierphant Publishing, 2012.

Messinger, JD. *11 Days in May.* Cardiff, CA: Waterfront Digital Press, 2012.

Millman, Dan. *The Four Purposes of Life.* Tiburon, CA: New World Press, 2011.

-*The Peaceful Warrior.* Novato, CA: New World Library, 1980.

Moody, Raymond, MD. *Life After Life.* New York: Harper Collins Publishing, 2001. MBB Inc., 1975.

-*Glimpses of Eternity.* USA: Guideposts, 2010.

Moorjani, Anita. *Dying to Be Me.* Carlsbad, CA: Hay House Inc., 2012.

Mora, Eva Maria. *Quantum Angel Healing.* Austin, TX: Synergy Books, 2012.

Moss, Richard, M.D. *Inside-Out Healing.* Carlsbad, CA: Hay House, 2011.

Namm, Edith. "Change to a Positive Mindset and Extend Your Lifeline." Bloomington, IN: Authorhouse, 2011.

Newbigging, Sandy. *Thunk.* Scotland, UK: Findhorn Press, 2012.

Nicholson, Ester. *Soul Recovery.* Culver City, CA: Agape Media International, 2013.

Pearce, Stewart. *The Angels of Atlantis.* Scotland, UK: Findhorn Press, 2011.

-*The Alchemy of Voice.* Scotland, UK: Findhorn Press, 2010.

Pearl, Eric, D.C. *The Reconnection.* Carlsbad, CA: Hay House Inc., 2001.

About the Author

Sheryl Glick is a certified Reiki Master Teacher, an energy healer, and spiritual medium who offers individual and group sessions and is a teacher of the techniques of healing and spiritual and intuitive psychic development. She is a member of the International Association of Reiki Professionals, as well as a long-time hospice volunteer.

Before her work in energy healing, Sheryl was a teacher for elementary school and special needs children in New York City and holds a BA and MS in education and literature.

She is the author of *Life Is No Coincidence: The Life and Afterlife Connection,* and has worked with prominent speakers and visionaries who are seeking to awaken us to greater self-awareness and appreciation of our inner soul being and physical life.

Sheryl is also the host of *Healing from Within,* an Internet radio show on Web Talk Radio and Dream Visions 7 Radio Network. She can be heard at www.sherylglick.com, www.webtalkradio.net, and www.dreamvisions7radio.com. Sheryl and her guests explore the many facets of universal energy healing and the aligning of our physical and inner being for a complete, healthy, and dynamic human experience, and encourage the most loving ways for us to reach out to each other as we develop into more civilized and conscientious human beings.

Sheryl Glick opens her mind and heart to help awaken in others a higher view of our life experience through shared coincidences, synchronistic happenings, and miracles.

For more information about
The Living Spirit: Answers to Healing and Infinite Love
visit
www.sherylglick.com